AWASH WITH COLOR

WATERCOLOR WALL QUILTS

Step-by-Step Instructions Included

JUDY TURNER

Good Books™

Intercourse, PA 17534
800/762-7171
www.goodbks.com

D1451570

DEDICATION

To my parents, Joan and John Hepburn, who in their individual ways have taught me to cherish every moment.

JMT

EDITORIAL

MANAGING EDITOR
Judy Poulos
EDITORIAL ASSISTANT
Ella Martin
EDITORIAL COORDINATOR
Margaret Kelly

PHOTOGRAPHY

Andrew Payne
STYLING
Kathy Tripp

PRODUCTION AND DESIGN

MANAGER
Anna Maguire
LAYOUT
Lulu Dougherty
COVER DESIGN/DESIGN & PRODUCTION COORDINATOR
Cheryl Dubyk-Yates
CONCEPT DESIGN
Jenny Pace

Printed in Hong Kong

North American edition published by Good Books, 2002. All rights reserved.

Original edition published in English under the title *Awash With Color*
by J.B. Fairfax Press Pty Limited., Rushcutters Bay, Australia, 1997.

AWASH WITH COLOR

Copyright © 2002 by Good Books, Intercourse, PA 17534
International Standard Book Number: 1-56148-373-7
Library of Congress Catalog Card Number: 2002073851

Library of Congress Cataloging-in-Publication Data

Turner, Judy
    Awash with color : watercolor wall quilts : step-by-step instructions included /
Judy Turner.
    p.cm.
    ISBN 1-56148-373-7
    1. Patchwork--Patterns. 2. Watercolor quilting. 3. Patchwork quilts. I. Title.

TT835.T792 2002
746.46--dc21   2002073851

Contents

Introduction

While I was growing up, it seemed to me that my mother could make anything she wanted with her hands. Apart from making all our clothes, she did exquisite embroidery and wonderful knitting. I clearly remember seeing boxes of beautifully made dolls' clothes ready for the school festival. She was a regular student at the local technical college, studying dressmaking, interior decorating, upholstery, soft furnishings, floral arrangement, basketry and cake decorating. Years later, I joined her in pottery and gourmet cooking classes, as well as attending dressmaking and soft furnishing classes myself. Her talents decorated our home and extended to the garden. It is no accident that my sister, Barbara Gower, and I share a love of needlework and gardens. At a young age, we were encouraged to make clothes for our dolls, as well as for ourselves. My mother's practical approach to problem-solving and the enormous amount she learned by creating with her hands provided a wonderful role model for me. Her two sisters, Alison Harrison and Nancy Jenkins, shared all my mother's talents, and they too opened my eyes to the pleasure and sense of achievement that needlework could provide.

It was in 1980, while visiting my Aunt Alison, that I first became interested in patchwork. A cushion she had made caught my attention, so she promptly sketched the design, enabling me to make it on my own when I returned home. My attempt was a disaster! I thought it would be like dressmaking – taking the seams in or letting them out until the pieces fitted. I had tried to make the block without templates. Still interested in attempting patchwork, I enrolled in classes with Margaret Rolfe and Wendy Saclier, two well-known Australian quilters. The enthusiasm shared in that first class remains with me still.

Many events and people have influenced my work over the years. Between 1981 and 1983, I made nine traditional quilts. The video *Quilts in Women's Lives* (1983) was a turning point for me. In the video, one quilter arranges triangles of blue and white printed fabric from light to dark on a felt wall. In no time my husband had build a felt wall in our bedroom. My first blended-print quilt, "Ashes of Roses," using quick-pieced triangles, soon followed.

Although there were no books available on the subject, I realized I would need to piece lights with lights, lights with mediums, mediums with mediums, mediums with darks, and darks with darks – to blend the fabrics in a wash of color, just as an artist would with paint and brush.

In 1984 my mother gave me a rotary cutter and cutting mat, enabling me to make my son a Log Cabin quilt in just one week. I enjoyed working with strips, and made my first pictorial quilt, "Daybreak Island," in the same year by blending printed strips of fabric on my felt wall until I had created a picture.

Since that time, I have continued to work with strips, as well as multiple-piecing (Four-patch, Nine-patch, Rail-fence), using printed fabric and blending the colors on my felt wall. By not working in single units, there is always the element of surprise when a splash of light appears in a dark area or a dark note in a light area. To date, I have not found the need to redo a section of piecing, enjoying each surprise and its contribution to the finished quilt. Since the late eighties, the availability of large prints and multicolored fabrics has made it possible for me to make more colorful quilts.

Although my mother has been my strongest influence, many other talented people have also influenced my work. These include the impressionists, particularly Claude Monet and the Australian artist, Fred Williams; Kaffe Fassett, for his use of color, and Deidre Amsden, whose colorwash quilts are well known throughout the world.

Ideas for my quilt designs have come from visual and emotional experiences, as well as from photos, gift wrap, the garden, or simply a beautiful piece of fabric. Often one quilt develops from another. The more quilts I make, the more I learn, and ideas come flooding at a faster rate than I can possibly sew.

I owe an enormous debt to my students. Their enthusiasm has encouraged me to find creative solutions – often on the spot – teaching me more than I would ever have learned had I worked in isolation. The rewards have been in the many friendships I have formed, as well as in witnessing my students' creative growth and confidence with color. Perhaps the most satisfying thing of all has been to see my daughter's enjoyment of stitching, thus continuing the thread into the next generation.

Awash with Color Basics

We live in a wonderful, colorful world, a fact that is often not fully appreciated. Inspiration for many of the quilts in this book comes from the observation of my surroundings and an understanding of the importance of color value. Color observation and knowledge of the types of fabrics which will be easier to blend are crucial in the making of these quilts. Information about color and fabric appears in the following section, which describes as simply as possible how to collect fabrics for watercolor quilts and how to arrange them to see if you have achieved the required flow of color.

The Technical Details section provides all the information you need to make a well-finished quilt, including very important tips for working with strips. Various tools and types of equipment are also helpful in assisting with the blending of color, and these are also described here.

Read Awash with Color Basics carefully, before beginning any of the projects in this book.

Choosing Colors and Fabrics

MY COLORFUL WORLD

As a child, I always wished I could paint. While still in school I attended Saturday morning watercolor classes, a subject which I pursued again briefly some 10 years ago. Several color workshops over the years only added to my frustration in truly understanding color, its various terms and relationships. Most of what I have learned about color, I have learned from simple observation and practice.

The environment in which I live has had an enormous impact on my appreciation of color. Canberra is a city which experiences exciting seasonal changes which simply cannot be ignored in daily life. Added to this,

constant visits of wild parrots outside my studio have heightened my appreciation of color and my surroundings.

It was in the late eighties, after losing a close friend and my mother, that I began to see everything more clearly, to observe and absorb color in a way I had not done before – to cherish each moment. At the same time, I began to teach widely throughout Australia, holding the colors I experienced in my head for future use. During my travels I observed that quilters worked well with colors from their immediate environment, and not so well with colors that didn't surround them in nature.

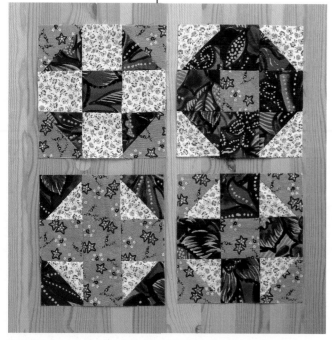

Detail 1: The same pattern can be changed to look quite different by changing the value of the shapes within it

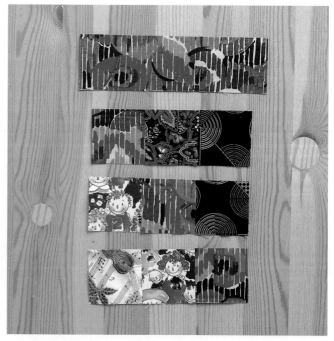

Detail 2: The same fabric can appear to be light, medium or dark, depending on the value of the fabrics around it

Wherever you live or travel, look more closely at nature's way of pulling colors together. By absorbing what you see, you will have your own personal color memory to use in your quilts.

COLOR VALUE

Color value refers to the lightness or darkness of color. Making a blended print quilt will be an exercise in learning about the relative value of color, even when many different colors are used. Many patchwork patterns, such as Log Cabin, rely on value to create the design. If the blocks were the same value, rather than half of them being light and half being dark, it would be impossible to create Barn-raising or Streak of Lightning designs from Log Cabin blocks. A pattern can be changed by changing the value of the shapes within it. See how the same shapes in different values can create a different pattern (detail 1).

Contrast can easily be achieved by placing light next to dark, but it's the medium range of value that provides the key to a quilt's success. Once you have learned to blend color from light to dark, you will see endless opportunities for using this knowledge in your quiltmaking.

Colors are of a high value if they have a large amount of white added: for example, powder blue. They are of low value if they have a lot of black added, as in navy blue, with many different values or shades in between. Color value is relative. A fabric can appear to be light, medium, or dark, depending on the value or depth of color of the fabrics that surround it (detail 2).

Most successful quilts contain light, medium, and dark values in varying amounts. In "Reef Wash" (page 42), a few medium blocks have been used in either light or dark positions, adding interest to the quilt. The quilts in this book use light, medium, and dark value fabrics in different ways. "Simply Blue" (page 30), "Winter Surprise" (page 72) and "Reef Wash" (page 42) do not require a full gradation of color as they rely on light/dark contrast. However, the inclusion of medium fabrics adds interest to each quilt. "Autumn" (page 20), "Spring" (page 51), "Summer" (page 56), "Moonlight and Roses" (page 35), "Colorwash Cascade" (page 60), and "Black Jewel" (page 66) rely on a full gradation of color for maximum effect.

COLLECTING FABRICS

Although I prefer to use one hundred percent cotton fabrics, I would use polyester/cotton blends if the color was what I needed. One hundred percent cotton fabrics are preferable because they press flat and do not shrink if the iron is too hot. I use a combination of patchwork, dressmaking, and decorator fabrics.

A simple way to begin collecting fabrics for a blended print quilt is to start with one favorite fabric that contains many colors, and to consider using any fabric that doesn't scream at this one fabric. Look beyond the obvious color of the fabric and try to use fabrics containing any or many of the colors in the first fabric. Include prints of different scales, such as tiny prints, large prints, and scattered prints. Previously rejected fabric,

Detail 3: The wrong side of some fabrics can also be used and will increase your range of available fabrics

odd colors, or dated fabrics often work well. To fabrics already in your personal store add some of the latest prints available for a stunning effect. The wrong side of some fabrics can be used, as well as the right side (detail 3).

For this type of quilt, avoid solids, stripes, large checks, and tone-to-tone fabrics (detail 4). Collect a variety of prints, including florals of various sizes and multicolored prints with a splash of light – the busier the print the better.

Busy, splashy prints (detail 5) are the easiest to use. Muddy fabrics (detail 6) are more difficult. When you begin making blended print quilts, it is easier to use all the same kind of fabrics, for example, checks or florals, but with experience, most fabrics can be mixed. As I wish to collect a large variety of fabrics, I usually only purchase 12 in (30 cm) of each fabric, unless I see endless possibilities or border potential in a stunning print, which might lead me to purchase as much as 3¼ yd (3 m).

Many shades of one color are easier to use than a mixture of colors from light to dark, if you have not made a blended print quilt before (see "Simply Blue" on page 30). With experience and the wide availability of multicolored fabrics, you will enjoy the challenge of mixing many colors to make a new color, just as an artist does with paint and brush.

If you remember the colors you have observed throughout your life, you will have your own color memory to draw on, adding to the pleasure of making and sharing your quilt.

EVALUATING THE FABRICS

Line up the fabrics from light to dark so you can see the same amount of each fabric (detail 7). Shift the position of fabrics as necessary until you have a flow of color. Use value-determining tools to help you to decide the exact position of each fabric and to help you see any trouble spots (see page 16). Eliminate any fabrics that stand out. If the overall coloring looks better without a certain fabric, leave it out. Don't forget that some fabrics may need to be reversed to fit within the flow of color that you have

Detail 4 (Left): Tone-on-tone fabrics are difficult to use in a watercolor quilt
Detail 5 (Middle): Busy, splashy prints are the easiest to use
Detail 6 (Right): Muddy fabrics are more difficult to blend

arranged. If you don't have a range of fabrics that blend at this stage, you won't have when the quilt is pieced, so keep searching until you have filled the gaps where the jump in value is too great. Time spent at this stage is invaluable. A fresh look on another day always works wonders. With practice, you will be able to look at the fabrics and see the depth of color, rather than the color itself. Remember, a more subtle gradation is possible when you use a very large number of different fabrics.

ARRANGING THE FABRICS
Yardage amounts

It is impossible to determine exact yardage amounts for many of the quilt tops in this book, such as "Autumn" (page 20), "Spring" (page 51), and "Summer" (page 56). For these quilts, strips are cut in varying widths, and scraps and decorating samples are often used. Sometimes a section of strip will need to be cut out because a solid area has appeared between the printed areas. As a guide, if you have for the top twice the amount of fabric that has been determined for the back, you will have plenty. The wonderful thing about making a blended print quilt is that you can substitute or add extra fabrics at any time.

Detail 7: Line up your fabrics with the same amount of each one showing until you have a flow of color

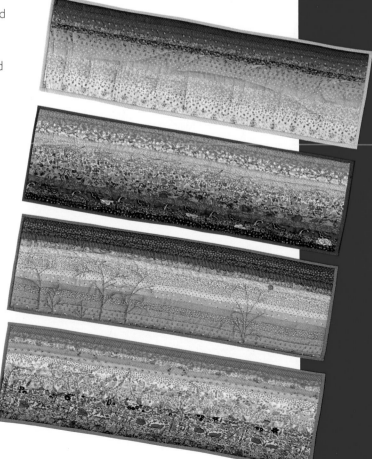

Right: CANBERRA SEASONS
Judy Turner
Each panel is 10 in x 32 in
(25 cm x 81 cm)

11

Technical Details

MEASUREMENTS

Both imperial and metric measurements are used in this book. These measurements are not interchangeable; therefore it is important to use one or the other (imperial or metric) in any one quilt. Figures have been rounded off to the most useful equivalent to avoid the use of excessively difficult numbers. The measurements have been carefully adjusted to ensure that the quilt goes together well.

ROTARY CUTTING TIPS

Iron any creases out of the fabric first, then fold the fabric double with selvages matching. Cut the left-hand edge in one of the following ways:

1   Line up the fold in the fabric parallel to the top and bottom lines on your mat. With the ruler on the left-hand side, lined up with the grid, cut along the right-hand edge of the fabric.
2   Use a small square ruler on the fold of the fabric, lined up to the left-hand edge of a long ruler which is just covering the raw edges of the fabric. Cut along the right-hand edge after removing the small square ruler.

Apply the reverse procedures, if you are left-handed. When you are cutting, always apply firm pressure with your hand on the ruler to stop it from slipping. Keep your fingers well clear. Make sure the blade is covered when the cutter is not in use.

SEAM ALLOWANCES AND STITCH LENGTH

It is important for seam allowances to remain consistent throughout your project, using either a ¼ in or 7.5 mm seam allowance. Please note, these measurements are not interchangeable.

For some projects I suggest a smaller than usual stitch (for example, 2 instead of 2.5), because the pieces have been rotary cut, there is no back-tracking, and some of the quilts are large and heavy when being handled or pressed. A smaller stitch will strengthen the quilt and prevent the stitching from coming undone during handling.

Where possible, seam allowances should be pressed together in alternate directions to allow the seams to butt together when the rows are being joined. If this is not possible, for example, as in "Moonlight and Roses" (page 35), line up the seams as best you can by stacking the seam allowances one on top of the other.

When your quilt top is completed, staystitch close to the outside edges to prevent the seams from coming undone and the edges from stretching.

TIPS FOR SEWING STRIPS

It is important to sew strips in alternate directions to avoid stretching the fabric. If you leave a tail of thread where you begin sewing and cut the thread off neatly where you finish sewing, you will always know where you began. If possible, sew strips in groups of two, then the groups of two into groups of four, and so on. This will help to prevent overhandling, which can also stretch the fabric.

With many quilts in this book, you will, in a sense, be making your own fabric, then cutting it up in a variety of ways. It is possible to cut the stretch out of the fabric by restraightening the cut edge, where necessary, as you go.

Fabric can become stretched while being joined, because of different weaves and various weights. If you are still having trouble, pin before you begin to sew.

TIPS FOR BORDERS

The border strips for quilts in this book have been cut slightly longer than necessary to allow for differences in actual piecing. Fabric requirements for the borders, given with each quilt, allow for borders to be cut in one piece. If you wish to purchase less fabric, you will need to join the border strips. Add borders to the long sides first.

ADDING BORDERS

1 Measure each border through the center of the quilt, using the cut border strip instead of a tape measure.
2 Pin-mark where the border strips match the sides of the quilt. Fold the border strip until the pins match and mark the center. Fold the strip again and pin-mark it into quarters.
3 Fold the length of the quilt into quarters and pin-mark. Match the pins in the quilt and the border.
4 Pin the border to the quilt with a pin every 4 in (10 cm), with the points of the pins facing the raw edges. Always stitch with the larger piece (usually the quilt) underneath.
5 Press the seam towards the border. Cut off the excess fabric using a rotary cutter and ruler placed square on the edge of the quilt and border.
6 Repeat these steps for the other borders.

PREPARATION FOR MACHINE-QUILTING

Backing

Make the quilt backing at least 2 in (5 cm) larger all around than the quilt top. Join the backing in the most economical way possible, either with seams across the quilt or down the length of the quilt. Press the seams open.

Batting

The quilt-as-you-go designs in this book require a thin, firm, bonded batting. All the other quilts require a low-loft batting. Cut the batting the same size as the backing. If the batting needs to be joined, simply butt two clean-cut edges together and oversew by hand, keeping the join flat.

Layering the quilt

1 Spread the quilt backing on a large flat surface (a ping pong table or the floor will work well) with the wrong side up. Secure the backing to the table with masking tape or pin it to the carpet to keep it flat.
2 Position the batting on top of the backing, making sure it is flat and smooth.
3 Press the quilt top well and center it on top of the batting with the right side up. Smooth out the top, from the center to the edges.
4 Pin-baste the quilt with 1½ in (4 cm) safety pins approximately every 3 in (7.5 cm), pinning from the center to the edges. If you close the pins as you go you may disturb the layers, so leave the pins open until the entire quilt has been pin-basted. Turn the quilt over and check for wrinkles before closing all the pins. If you own a pin closer, you can close the pins as you go.

MACHINE-QUILTING

All the quilts in this book have been machine-quilted. Because fabrics of various weights have been used, including decorator fabrics, and because there are many seam allowances to stitch through, machine-quilting is a practical solution.

1 To set up for machine-quilting, you will need a clear workspace with a small table (a card table works well) on your left-hand side to support the quilt. Use a walking foot on your sewing machine, if you have one.
2 Using scraps of batting and fabric, make a sample to test your stitching. You may need to adjust the stitch length to get a normal length stitch through the batting, especially if you don't have a walking foot. If you are using monofilament thread, you may need to loosen the top tension to achieve an even stitch.

3 Mark the quilting lines with a chalk wheel where necessary, preparing only a few rows at a time so the chalk won't wear off before you quilt that area.

4 Begin quilting from the center of the outside edge for straight quilting, or from the corners for diagonal quilting. Quilt from the center out when the central panel is quilted before the border is quilted, as in "Outback Safari" (page 47).

5 Roll the half of the quilt that you intend to quilt first and position it under the arm of the machine. For straight line or diagonal quilting, quilt half the quilt in one direction before rolling the opposite side and repeating the procedure.

6 When the quilting is completed, trim the excess backing and batting from the edge of the quilt.

Hand-quilting is another option for the quilts in this book. However, small stitches would be difficult to achieve because of the vast number of seam allowances to sew across. To prepare for hand-quilting, layer the quilt in the same way as for machine-quilting, then baste the layers together by hand in a 6 in (15 cm) grid.

BINDING

Note: The specific cut size of the binding is given for each quilt.

1 Fold the strips in half lengthwise, with the wrong sides together, and press.

2 Measure through the center of the quilt as for the borders. Add the binding to the long sides first. Pin the binding to the right side of the quilt, with all the raw edges together, pinning every 4 in (10 cm) with the points of the pins facing the raw edges.

3 Stitch the binding in place, then blind-stitch the binding on the back by hand.

4 When adding binding to the short sides of the quilt, allow an extra 1 in (2.5 cm) at each end. This extra fabric will be folded to cover the corners, before blind-stitching on the back by hand.

SIGNING YOUR QUILT

The finishing touch to every quilt should include a label to provide important details for future recipients. Details should include the maker's name and year of completion, but could also include the address or location, inspiration, intended recipient's name, and any other relevant details. Labels can either be embroidered by hand (I use backstitch), written with a waterproof fabric marker, or embroidered with a computerized sewing machine.

Left: An interesting and creative label is the perfect finishing touch for a quilt

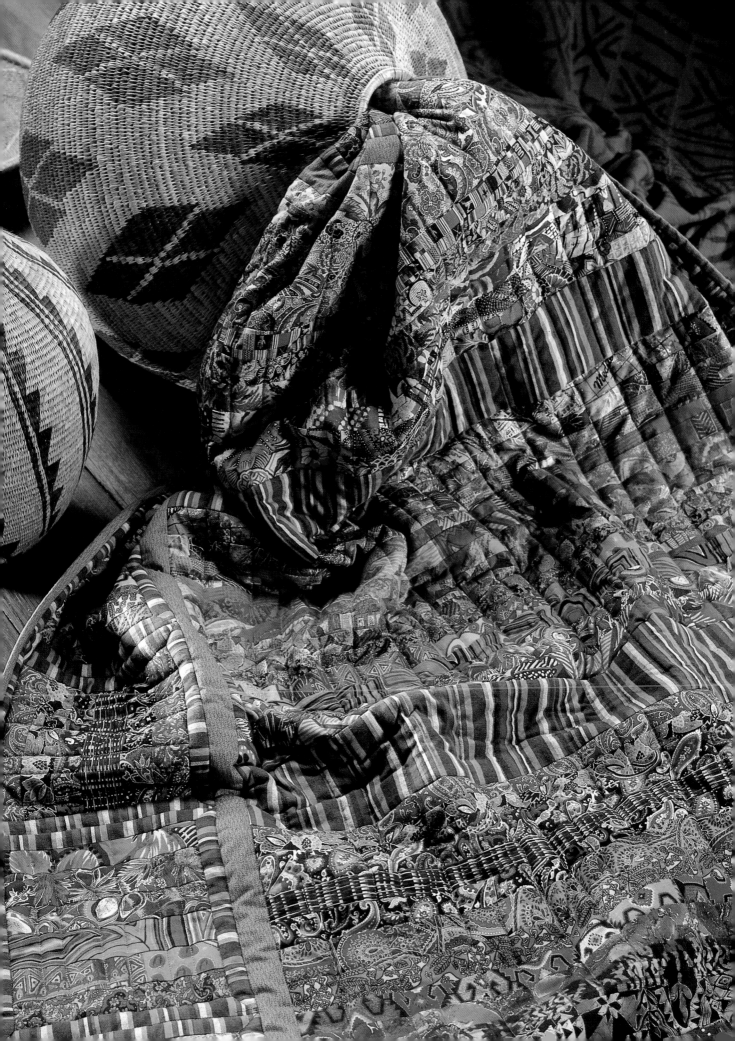

Tools and Equipment

VERTICAL WORK SURFACE

A vertical work surface or a design wall is an essential piece of equipment which enables you to experiment with your blocks or strips and allows you to change the pieces to achieve the best results. My current design wall is a screen which consists of several 4 ft x 8 ft (1.2 m x 2.4 m) sheets of pin-board material, covered in white felt and surrounded with timber. Each screen is free-standing and can be readily moved. I often use them side by side for a large project. Because the screens are resting against a wall, the fabric pieces are even less likely to fall because of the angle of the screen. If you don't have a large workspace, a similar surface can easily be made by pinning a flannel sheet or a piece of Pellon to the wall or curtains.

VALUE-DETERMINING TOOLS

Value-determining tools will help visually to remove the individual fabrics and show where there is a jump in value – a trouble spot. By reducing the image they will help you to focus on these problem areas. Your eyes are the best tools you have in helping you to determine value. If your eyesight is good, you can squint to reduce the image; if it is poor, simply take your glasses off for the same effect.

The following tools will help you to determine the value of your fabrics as you are trying to arrange them:
- A reducing glass is the opposite of a magnifying glass and will put distance visually between you and your work.
- A peephole, usually used in a door, is my favorite tool. Readily available at any hardware store, this little tool will reduce your work even more than a reducing glass. Good eyesight is necessary for this tool to work.
- A pair of binoculars used backwards will also reduce your work.
- A camera is another tool which works like a reducing glass. Photos also reduce the image, highlighting any problem areas.
- Photocopying your fabric will take away the color completely. By producing shades of black, white and grey, it is easier to see the value of fabrics in relation to one another. Transparent red plastic has a similar effect to photocopying, but is not as clear. I find these two methods the least useful, as they take away the color completely, and my main objective is to mix color as much as possible.

ROTARY CUTTER AND SELF-HEALING MAT

A rotary cutter and mat are essential for making the quilts in this book. The accuracy and speed this equipment provides has changed the face of quiltmaking.

RULERS

You need a selection of square rulers, as well as a long ruler, to use in conjunction with the rotary cutter and mat. The quilt-as-you-go blocks in this book are cut back using a square ruler and rotary cutter.

STEAM IRON

A steam iron is essential for pressing pieces flat, particularly where many strips are joined together.

CHALK WHEEL

My favorite tool for marking quilting lines is a chalk wheel, which is available in many different brands and in a variety of colors. It is important to have white for marking dark fabric, and a color that will show when marking light fabric. Mark only a short distance at a time because the chalk will wear off.

PIN CLOSER

A pin closer helps prevent the layers of the quilt from shifting while you are pinning them together and prevents sore fingers from the action of closing the pins.

SAFETY PINS

Safety pins, approximately 1½ in (4 cm) long, are ideal for securing the layers of the quilt in preparation for machine-quilting.

OTHER EQUIPMENT

Other usual equipment, such as a sewing machine, scissors, pins, needles and thread, will also be required.

Left: You will need a selection of the items pictured, including a sewing machine, rotary cutter and mat, rulers, value-determining tools, chalk wheel and safety pins

Awash with Color Quilts

For this book, I have made quilts in various sizes, including queen-size, double-bed-size, single-bed-size, lap and cot quilts. Although I have made many wall quilts in the past, I have always enjoyed making bed quilts. In the future, I am sure it will be the bed quilts that will be handed down, offering comfort and a link with the past to each new owner.

The availability of a huge range of fabrics suitable for quiltmaking has created a new breed of obsessive collector known in the quilt world as a "fabricaholic." If you are one, these quilts will help you clear your fabric stash so you can justify starting all over again. For those who have recently caught this bug, here is your opportunity to collect from the wide range of fabrics readily available to add to what you already have in store.

All the quilts in this book are made without templates by using a rotary cutter and streamlined piecing techniques. Apart from "Black Jewel" on page 66, all the piecing is from simple strips, using a large variety of fabrics. This gives you the opportunity to use scraps remaining from previous projects, as well as newly purchased yardage.

I have aimed to address both the beginner and the advanced quilter, who would like to make a scrap quilt by blending color. The quilts in this book range from simple designs to the more complex, giving you the opportunity to combine many fabrics and, by doing so, to learn the importance of color value.

Autumn

YOU WILL NEED

Note: All fabric quantities are calculated on 44 in (112 cm) wide fabric.

- assorted light, medium, and dark fabrics for the blocks
- 2½ yd (2.3 m) of dark print fabric for the seam-covering strips and binding for the front
- 2½ yd (2.3 m) of dark print fabric for the seam-covering strips and binding for the back

Note: If you wish to use the same seam-covering fabric for the front and the back, you will need a total of 5 yd (4.6 m) of fabric.

- 6¼ yd (5.7m) of fabric for the backing
- 9¼ yd (8.4 m) of thin, firm batting, 29 in (74 cm) wide
- sewing machine
- rotary cutter, mat, and ruler
- thread to blend with the fabrics
- thread to match the backing fabric
- large and small square rulers
- a few glass-headed pins

Finished size: 78 in x 90 in (195 cm x 225 cm)
Finished size of each block: 6 in (15 cm)
Total number of blocks: 195

The colors I have chosen for this quilt reflect the rich colors of fall – my favorite season. The design for "Autumn" is a variation of a quilt I made in 1989. The idea to use a straight grid and diagonal coloring came from gift-wrapping paper. The fabric for the seam-covering strip on the front was a starting point for collecting all other fabrics. As this fabric is of medium value, it appears to be light at the bottom of the quilt, disappears in the center, and appears to be dark at the top of the quilt. A very wide range of fabrics, from light to dark, make a rich, multicolored combination when joined.

Note: A zigzag stitch on your machine is essential for the construction of this quilt.

INSTRUCTIONS
Cutting

1   Arrange your fabrics from light to dark. Beginning with the darkest fabrics, cut a selection of strips, varying in width from 1–2 in (2.5–5 cm). As you make the blocks, you will cut extra strips.

2   From the backing fabric, cut from selvage to selvage thirty-three strips, 6¾ in (17 cm) wide. Cross-cut the strips into 195 squares.

3   From the batting, cut forty-nine strips 6¾ in (17 cm) wide. Cross-cut them into 195 squares.

4   From the seam-covering/binding fabric cut from selvage to selvage:
   • fifty-two strips 1¼ in (3.5 cm) wide, to cover the front seams;
   • fifty-two strips 1¼ in (3.5 cm) wide, to cover the back seams;
   • eight strips 1¼ in (3.5 cm) wide, for the front binding;
   • eight strips 1¾ in (4.5 cm) wide, for the back binding.

MAKING THE BLOCKS

Note: Use ¼ in (7.5 mm) seam allowances.

1   Begin working in the bottom right-hand corner of the quilt, using the darkest fabrics and make one block at a time. Pin

Detail 1: Position the first cut strip diagonally across the batting

Detail 2: Stitch the first two strips together through all layers

AUTUMN
Judy Turner

Detail of "Autumn," showing the grid formed by the strips on the back of the quilt

4 Continue adding strips in the same manner until that side of the square is covered with strips, then turn the square and continue adding strips in the same manner until the square is completely covered (detail 4).

5 Cover a total of 195 squares. It is important to blend the colors as you add the strips. Cut more strips of varying widths as you need them.

6 Trim each block by turning it over and cutting away to the edge of the backing fabric (detail 5). Using a square ruler trim each block to a 6 in (15 cm) square. Make sure the diagonal line on the ruler is parallel with the seams. As each block is completed, pin it to the vertical work surface. This will help you see what depth of color is needed next.

Assembling the quilt

1 When all the blocks have been made and arranged on the vertical work surface to your satisfaction, you are ready to assemble the quilt. The quilt is fifteen blocks long by thirteen blocks wide. The diagonal strips should all be running in the same direction.

2 Cross-cut twenty-six of the 1¼ in (3.5 cm) wide front seam-covering strips into 6 in (15 cm) lengths, until you have a total of 182 short strips. The remaining

the 6¾ in (17 cm) squares of batting to the same size squares of backing fabric, with the pins on the batting side, and the wrong side of the fabric facing the batting.

2 Position the first strip diagonally across the batting (detail 1).

3 Position the second strip on top of the first strip, with the right sides together. Stitch down the right-hand side (detail 2). Make sure the strips are long enough to cover the batting when the top strip is turned back towards the batting (detail 3). Finger-press the seam.

Detail 3: Make sure the strips are long enough to cover the batting when the top strip is turned back

Detail 4: Continue adding strips in the same manner until the square of batting is completely covered

twenty-six 1¼ in (3.5 cm) wide strips will be joined as needed for long strips on the front.

3   Repeat step 2 with the 1¼ in (3.5 cm) wide back seam-covering strips.

Constructing the quilt

1   Join the blocks in vertical rows in the following way: Pin a 1¼ in x 6 in (3.5 cm x 15 cm) strip to both sides of the bottom edge of each block and stitch through all layers (detail 6). Do the same for the bottom edge of every block, except the last row.

2   On the opposite side of each block, stitch the width of the machine foot (detail 6). This will give you a consistent size to turn the seam-covering strip to.

3   Join the blocks by butting the seam allowances together and zigzag stitch with the widest zigzag stitching (detail 7). When the row is joined, turn it over and repeat the zigzag stitching on the back to add extra strength.

4   Fold the seam-covering strip, turning the raw edge under until it just meets the previous stitching. Blindstitch the strip in place on both sides by hand. The width of this seam must be consistent for the entire quilt.

Detail 5: Turn each block over and trim to the edge of the backing, before cutting to a 6 in (9.5 cm) square

Detail 6: Pin a 1¼ in x 6 in (3.5 cm x 15 cm) strip to the bottom edge of each block and stitch through all layers

Detail 7: Join the blocks by butting the seam allowances together and zigzagging with the widest stitch

Detail 8: Align the rows of blocks, pinning at the junction of the seam-covering strips with two long glass-headed pins

5 Join all six vertical rows of blocks in the same manner.

6 When all the vertical rows are completed, join them in the same manner by stitching the long, previously cut seam-covering strips, both front and back, to the right-hand edge of the vertical rows. Along the left-hand side of each row, stitch the width of your machine foot.

7 Number the rows to avoid confusion. Align the rows of blocks as in step 3. Using two long glass-headed pins, pin at the junctions of the seam-covering strips (detail 8) and zigzag the rows together. Sew slowly over the pins to avoid breaking the machine needle. Do not forget to turn the work over and zigzag on the back for extra strength. Join the quilt into groups of two rows, then groups of four rows and so on until the entire quilt top is together. Hand-finish the front and back seams as you go.

TO FINISH
Binding

Note: A reversible binding has been used to finish this quilt. When completed, the binding will be the same width as the other finished strips.

1 Join the previously cut front and back binding strips so you have two lengths – two lots of four strips.

2 Press the back binding in half, with the wrong sides together.

3 Join the back binding to the front binding with the right sides together (detail 9).

4 Press on the seamline towards the wrong side of the front binding (detail 10).

5 Measure the prepared binding through the center of the quilt. Pin-mark both the binding and the quilt into quarters.

6 Pin the binding strips to the long sides of the quilt with the points of the pins facing the raw edge of the quilt. The right side of the binding should face the right side of the front of the quilt.

7 After the binding is sewn in place, turn the binding to the back, so the seam joining the bindings is on the very outside edge of the quilt.

8 Blindstitch the folded edge to the back of the quilt. The seam allowances will help to fill the binding.

9 For the short sides of the quilt repeat the steps above, allowing an extra 1 in (2.5 cm) at each end. This extra fabric will be folded to cover the corners, before blindstitching the binding on the back by hand.

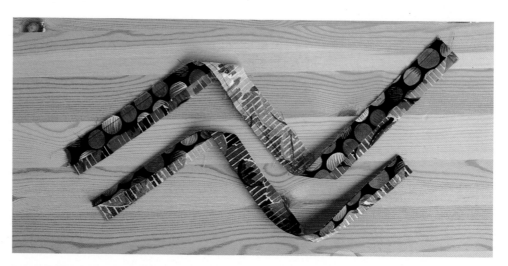

Detail 9 (Top): Join the back binding to the front binding with the right sides together
Detail 10 (Bottom): On the seamline, press the back binding to the wrong side of the front binding, so the seam lies exactly on the edge

Snowball

Finished size: 36½ x 48½ in
(91.5 cm x 121.5 cm)

This cot quilt is totally machine-made, stitched onto homespun and re-backed, making it a practical gift for a baby. It features a simple snowball block, made in the quilt-as-you-go technique, with light and medium prints contrasting with the dark blue fabric which frames each block.

If you wish to make a larger quilt, for example 72 in x 90 in (180 cm x 225 cm), you will need 180 blocks.

Note: A zigzag stitch on your machine is essential for the construction of this quilt.

INSTRUCTIONS
Cutting

1   From the assorted prints, cut strips in varying widths from 1¼–2 in (3.5–5 cm), from selvage to selvage.
2   From the plain, firm, dark cotton fabric, cutting lengthwise, cut:
    • ten strips, 1¼ in (3.5 cm) wide; from five of these strips, cut forty-two 6 in (15 cm) sections (the remaining strips are used for joining the vertical rows);
    • seven strips, 2 in (5 cm) wide, cross-cut into 192 squares;
    • four strips, 3½ in (9 cm) wide, for the binding.
3   From the calico or homespun, cutting crosswise, cut eight 6½ in (16.5 cm) wide strips, cross-cut into forty-eight squares.
4   From the batting, cut forty-eight 6½ in (16.5 cm) squares.

YOU WILL NEED
Note: All fabric quantities are calculated on 44 in (112 cm) wide fabric.
- assorted light and medium print fabrics
- 1⅝ yd (1.4 m) of plain, firm, dark cotton fabric
- 1⅝ yd (1.4 m) of homespun or well-washed calico
- 1½ yd (1.3 m) of fabric for the backing
- 2¼ yd (2 m) of thin, firm batting, 29 in (74 cm) wide
- sewing machine
- rotary cutter, mat, and ruler
- thread to blend with the fabrics
- thread to match the backing fabric
- large and small square rulers
- glass-headed pins

Detail 1: Pin a second strip in place, with right sides together, and stitch through all layers

Detail 2: Finger-press the second and subsequent strips so the right side is facing

25

To make the blocks

It is important to blend the colors to avoid a striped appearance. Place similar values side by side, or gradually add strips that are slightly darker. One side of the block will be a little darker than the other; this is preferable to mixing the values and creating a striped appearance and a busier quilt.

Note: Use ¼ in (7.5 mm) seam allowances.

1 Pin the 6½ in (16.5 cm) homespun squares to the same size batting squares.
2 Beginning on the left-hand side, place the first strip on the batting, right side up.
3 Place a second strip on top of the first strip, right sides together and with the raw edges on the right-hand side together. Pin it in place, then stitch the strips together, stitching through the batting and the backing (detail 1). Finger-press the second and subsequent strips so the right side is facing (detail 2). Add another strip in the same manner and continue until the square is completely covered (detail 3). Cover a total of forty-eight squares in this manner.

4 Trim all the blocks to 6 in (15 cm) using a square ruler and making sure the strips are parallel to the lines on the ruler (detail 4).
5 Stay-stitch the outside edges of each trimmed block (detail 4).
6 Press the dark squares in half, diagonally, with the wrong sides together.
7 Position the dark squares in each corner of each block and stitch along the pressed line (detail 5). Do not trim.
8 Fold the triangle out and stitch it down to the corner of the block (detail 5).
9 Pin all the blocks onto the vertical work surface, arranging them with the strips running in alternate directions.

Constructing the quilt

1 Pin a 1¼ in x 6 in (3.5 cm x 15 cm) strip to the bottom of the top left-hand side block. Stitch through all layers (detail 6).
2 Repeat the above procedure on the bottom of every block – except the last row of blocks.
3 Stitch along the opposite side of each block the width of the presser foot (detail

Detail 3: Continue adding strips until the square of batting is completely covered

Detail 4: Trim the blocks to 6 in (15 cm) and staystitch all the outside edges of each block

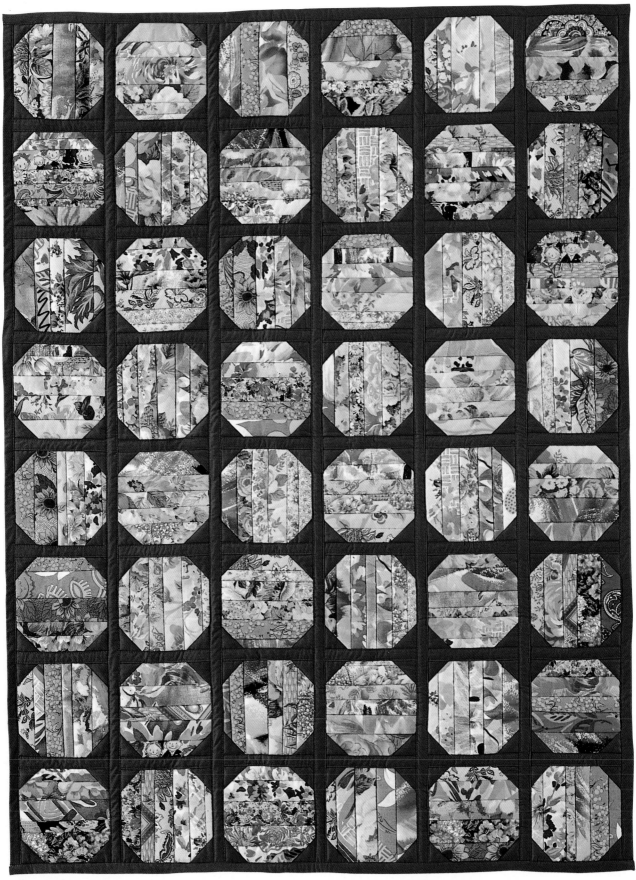

SNOWBALL
Judy Turner

6). This gives you a consistent distance to turn the seam-covering strip to.

4 Join the blocks by butting the seam allowances together and zigzag stitching in place with the widest zigzag stitching (detail 6). When the row is joined up, turn it over and repeat the zigzag stitching on the other side for extra strength.

5 Fold the seam-covering strip until it just meets previous stitching. Hand- or machine-finish. The width of this seam must be consistent for the entire quilt. If you are machine-finishing, stitch both sides close to the edge.

6 Join all six vertical rows of blocks in the same manner.

7 When all the vertical rows are completed, join them in the same manner as before by stitching the long previously-cut seam-covering strips to the right-hand edge of the vertical rows. Stitch along the left-hand side of each row, using the width of the presser foot as a guide, as before.

8 Align the rows of blocks, then join them by zigzagging, using two long glass-headed pins at the junction of the seam-covering strips (detail 7). Zigzag slowly, easing the horizontal blocks to fit the vertical blocks. Continue this procedure, pinning at each junction as you go. Sew slowly over the pins to avoid breaking the machine needle.

9 Repeat step 5. If the seam-covering strips are to be machine-finished, stitch down the right-hand edge only.

10 Position the quilt on the backing. Pin the backing and the quilt together.

11 If the seam-covering strips are machine-finished, attach the quilt to the backing by stitching the left-hand side of the vertical seam-covering strips, close to the edge. If the strips are hand-finished, tie through to the back of the quilt with strong thread by taking two small stitches through all the layers at the junction of the blocks. Tie the ends with a reef knot on the back of the work. Snip the threads, leaving a tail approximately ½ in (1.2 cm) long.

12 Trim the backing around the edge of the

 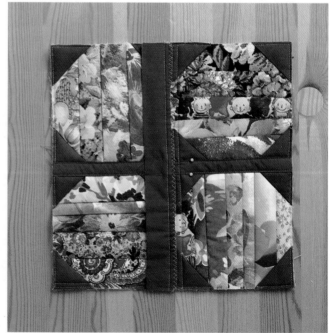

Detail 5 (Left): Press the dark squares in half, then stitch and fold them out to make the corners of the block
Detail 6 (Right): Pin and stitch the 6 in (15 cm) strips in place

Detail 7: Align the rows of blocks, matching seams. Join them by zigzag stitching, pinning at the junction of the seam-covering strips as you sew

quilt, leaving ¾ in (2 cm) of backing all around. Fold the backing to the quilt edge until it just covers the edge. Stay-stitch the backing in place. This will give some filling to a wider than usual binding.

TO FINISH
Binding

1   Fold the four previously cut 3½ in (9 cm) wide strips in half lengthwise, and press.

2   Measure through the center of the quilt as for the borders. Add the binding to the long sides first. With all the raw edges at the edge of the quilt, sew the binding to the wrong side of the quilt. Machine-finish on the front. If you are hand-finishing the binding, sew the binding to the right side first, then blind-stitch on the back.

3   When adding binding to the short sides, allow an extra 1 in (2.5 cm) at each end. This extra fabric will be folded to cover the corners, before machine-finishing on the front or hand-finishing on the back.

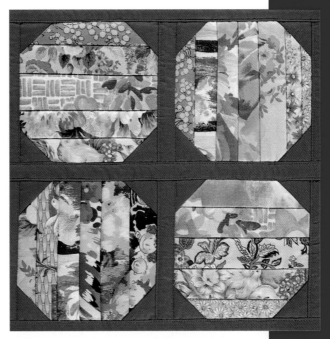

Above: Detail of "Snowball," showing the strips of splashy prints running vertically and horizontally

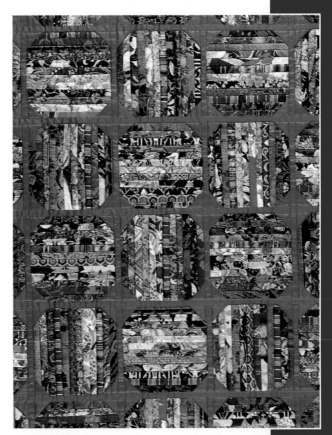

Above: Another version of "Snowball" which uses a 10 in (25 cm) block and the same-sized triangles to give a different effect

Simply Blue

YOU WILL NEED

Note: All fabric quantities are calculated on 44 in (112 cm) wide fabric.

- assorted light, medium, and dark fabrics for the rectangular blocks
- 2⅔ yd (2.4 m) of dark print fabric for the borders and binding
- 6 yd (5.4 m) of fabric for the backing
- 68 in x 115 in (167 cm x 270 cm) of batting
- sewing machine
- rotary cutter, mat, and ruler
- thread to blend with the fabrics
- thread to match the backing
- large square ruler
- chalk wheel
- safety pins

Finished size: 64 in x 105 in (157 cm x 260 cm)

A collection of fabrics from cream, scattered with blue, to navy blue, has been used in this quilt, which relies on light/dark contrast with the medium blues adding interest.

This is a very simple beginner's project.

INSTRUCTIONS

Cutting

1 From the assorted prints, cut strips from selvage to selvage in varying widths from 1¼–2½ in (3.5–6 cm).
2 Arrange the strips from light to dark. Cut extra strips as required.

Making the fabric for the rectangles

Note: Use ¼ in (7.5 mm) seam allowances.
1 It is important to sew the strips in alternate directions to avoid stretching (see "Tips for Sewing Strips" on page 12).

Keep the fabric edges together at one end to avoid waste. Beginning with the light fabrics, join strips of varying widths until you have a section of fabric that is at least 10 in (25 cm) wide by the width of the fabric (detail 1).

2 Make eight pieces of light fabric and eight pieces of dark fabric in this way. Make sure you blend the color within each section to avoid a striped appearance. Use the medium fabrics next to the darkest lights or at the beginning of the light-darks.

Cutting the fabric

1 Cut the "sewn" fabric into 10 in (25 cm) squares (details 2 and 3). If the sewn fabric is a little stretched, straighten the cut edges as you go. This will enable you to cut the stretched part out of the fabric. Do this for each of the eight light and eight dark sections. Each sewn section will yield four squares.
2 From each sewn section, cut two squares in half vertically and two squares in half horizontally (details 4 and 5). From the eight light and eight dark sections, you

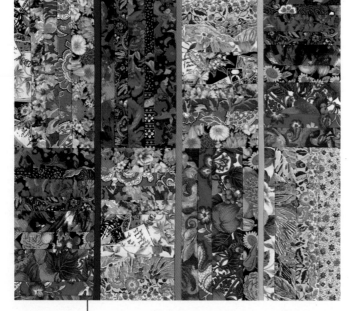

Above: The same pattern using a variety of bright colors separated by narrow strips looks quite different

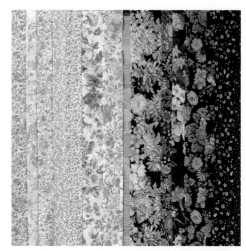

Detail 1: Join strips of varying widths until you have a section of fabric that is at least 10 in (25 cm) wide

SIMPLY BLUE
Judy Turner

will have thirty-two light and thirty-two dark squares, cut into rectangles to yield sixty-four light rectangles and sixty-four dark rectangles.

Note: You will use 120 rectangles altogether, giving you eight spare rectangles, so you can swap them around to get the most pleasing result.

Arranging the rectangles

1   Referring to the quilt photograph, arrange the rectangles on the vertical work surface with twelve rectangles across and ten rectangles down. Begin in the top left-hand corner with a dark vertical rectangle, then a light vertical rectangle, then a dark horizontal rectangle, then a light horizontal rectangle, and so on.

2   Row 2 will commence with a light horizontal rectangle, then a dark horizontal rectangle, then a light vertical rectangle, then a dark vertical rectangle, and so on (detail 6).

3   Move the blocks around until you are satisfied with the overall coloring.

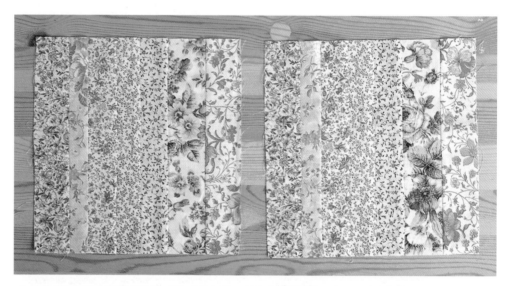

Details 2 and 3: Cut the light and dark sewn fabric into squares, like the ones above, for a total of sixty-four light and sixty-four dark squares

Joining the rectangles

1 Stack the blocks in rows, beginning at the bottom of the left-hand side. The top left-hand corner block will be on top. Put a pin in this block to mark the top corner of the quilt and leave the pin in place until the quilt is completed. Stack the second row, in the same manner, beginning at the bottom. From now on, it is safer to remove only one row at a time just prior to joining it to the other rows.

2 Beginning with the top two blocks from each stack, chain-piece them, using the same seam allowance as before. Little pinning should be necessary. Continue joining rows 1 and 2 in this manner. DO NOT CLIP THE THREADS.

3 Open up the sewn blocks and join the blocks from row 3 to the edge of row 2, in the same order. Join the quilt in four sections in this manner. After all the blocks are joined in vertical rows, the quilt should be held together by the thread between the rows of blocks.

4 Press the seams between the blocks together in one direction, and with each row of seams running in alternate directions.

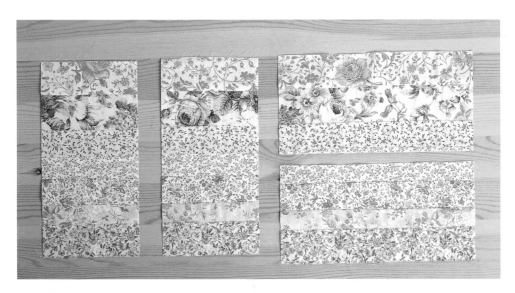

Details 4 and 5: From each sewn section, cut two squares in half vertically and two squares in half horizontally

Above: If you prefer, join the rows together with narrow strips of border fabric between

Note: If you prefer, you could join the rows vertically, then join the rows together with narrow strips of border fabric, cut 1 in (2.5 cm) wide. Take care to line up the rectangles horizontally as the narrow strips are added.

Joining the rows

1   Join the rows, without clipping the threads, by butting the seams between blocks. Sew slowly and stitch the rows in alternate directions to avoid stretching the fabric. When the four sections of the quilt are completed, join them together in vertical rows.
2   Staystitch ⅛ in (3 mm) from the outside edge of the entire quilt.

Borders

1   From the border fabric, cut four strips, 5½ in (14 cm) wide, down the length of the fabric.
2   To join on the borders, see the "Adding Borders" section in Technical Details on page 13.
3   Layer the completed quilt top with the batting and backing in preparation for machine-quilting.

QUILTING

1   See "Preparation for Machine-Quilting" (page 13). Ditch-stitch the quilt between the rectangles, both vertically and horizontally. Extend the lines through the borders with a chalk wheel, so the rows of quilting run through the border.
2   Mark with chalk through the center of the longest side of rectangles and through the border both sides. Quilt on these lines as well so a straight grid of squares appears on the surface.

TO FINISH
Binding

Cut four strips, 2½ in (6 cm) wide, on the straight grain. Join them, if necessary, to achieve the required length. To join on the binding see the "Binding" section in Technical Details on page 14.

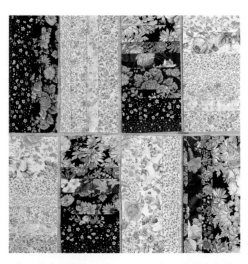

Detail 6: Arrange the rectangles with a dark vertical rectangle on the top left-hand corner, then a light vertical rectangle, and so on

Moonlight and Roses

Finished size: 104 in × 108 in
(244 cm × 254.5 cm)
**Finished size of each Nine-patch
block:** 4½ in (10.5 cm)
Total number of blocks: 420

Nine-patch blocks have been arranged to
represent a garden brimming with flowers
and lit by moonlight. I chose a collection of
very busy prints in colors which relate to
the border fabric.

Fabrics for a Nine-patch quilt

To achieve a blended effect, the fabrics
should be of low contrast and of light,
medium, and dark value. Solids, stripes, large
checks, and tone-on-tone fabrics are
unsuitable. Collect a variety of prints,
including florals of various sizes, and
multicolored prints with a splash of light –
the busier the print the better. Avoid muddy

prints. More than three-quarters of the
fabrics should be of dark and medium value.
For more information on choosing fabric see
page 9.

INSTRUCTIONS
Cutting

Cut three strips, 2 in (5 cm) wide, from
selvage to selvage, of each printed fabric.

Arranging the strips

1   Arrange the strips from light to dark
    with the same amount of each fabric
    showing. Shift the position of strips until
    you have a flow of color from light to
    dark (detail 1).
2   For the Nine-patch blocks, arrange the
    fabric strips into pairs. Beginning at the
    light end, start pairing the fabrics by
    moving up the range of values only as far
    as you need to. Within each pair, the

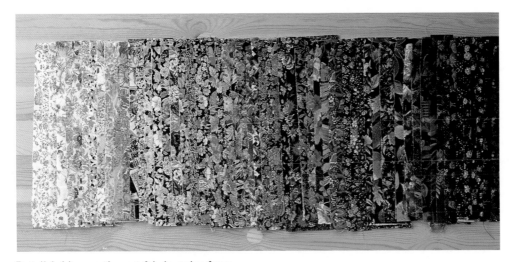

**Detail 1: Line up the cut fabric strips from
light to dark until there is a smooth flow of
color right across**

fabrics should be of a different scale, or one fabric should be just slightly darker than the other. Mix the colors as you are sorting them into pairs. If the fabrics are too similar, they will appear as one when they are joined. The blocks should appear to have nine small patches, not one large patch (detail 2). If you move from the light strips gradually to the dark strips, you will have automatically paired: light with light, light with medium, medium with medium, medium with dark, and dark with dark.

Sewing the strips

Note: Use ¼ in (7.5 mm) seam allowances and a smaller than usual stitch. This seam allowance MUST be consistent throughout the quilt.

1   Work with one set of fabrics at a time (that is, six strips), making sure the strips are the same length before you begin sewing. Sew two different strips together, with the right sides facing, then, without clipping the thread, sew the next two, making sure that a different fabric is on top. Add the third strip to the last pair you have sewn, then add the third strip to the other pair so the strips will have been sewn in alternate directions. This will give you twice three strips with the colors in alternate positions (detail 3). Press the seam allowances together in alternate directions within each set (detail 4). Place the completed sets flat, with the right sides together, until you are ready to cut them.

Cutting the sets into sections

On your cutting mat, line up across the width of the mat as many completed sets as your mat allows. Place them, still with the right sides together, and with the left-hand end of the sets in line. Square up the left-hand side of the completed sets, then cut them into 2 in (5 cm) sections, stacking them as you go, without flipping the sections over. Re-stack the sections in groups of three, turning every second group so the

Detail 2: The blocks should appear to have nine small patches, not one large patch, like the one on the left

Detail 3: Sew the strips into two groups of three with the colors in alternate positions in the sets

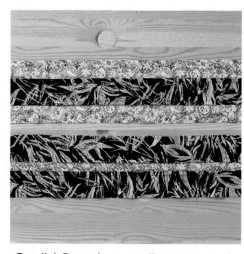

Detail 4: Press the seam allowances together in alternate directions within each set

MOONLIGHT AND ROSES
Judy Turner

Right: The shading of color is achieved with the placement of small Nine-patch blocks

right side of the outer section is facing, and piling them in a crisscross fashion (detail 5). Each group of three sections will make a block. You will have two different blocks from the same fabrics (detail 6). Each completed set should yield fourteen blocks.

Sewing the sections into blocks

1 Lift the first group of three sections from the pile. Place the first section right side down beside your machine. Chain-piece the other two sections together, butting seam allowances. Without clipping the threads, and making sure the first section

is also placed face down beside the machine, sew the next two sections; continue in this manner.

2 After these two sections of this set have been sewn, turn the pile of first sections over and, beginning where you started before, add them to complete the blocks (detail 7). Press the seams together in any direction.

Arranging the blocks

You will need to arrange the blocks carefully to achieve a blended effect. Stack all the blocks, keeping the same ones stacked together. Line up the blocks from light to dark. The shaded effect can be varied in many ways by shading light to dark, or dark to light, in one of several different directions (see photographs on pages 39 and 41).

Using the vertical work surface, begin in the center if the shading is from the center out, or at the top or bottom if the shading is diagonal or vertical.

While the alternate pressing of seams will allow for easier piecing, don't be concerned about breaking this rule while arranging the blocks, as you will have many more options if you ignore the directions in which the seams are pressed. Continue adding blocks that are increasingly darker or lighter in value until the quilt is twenty blocks across and twenty-one blocks long.

Detail 5: Stack the sections into groups of three, turning the top section of every second group so the right side is facing

Detail 6: Each group of three sections will make a block, and you will have two different blocks from the same fabric

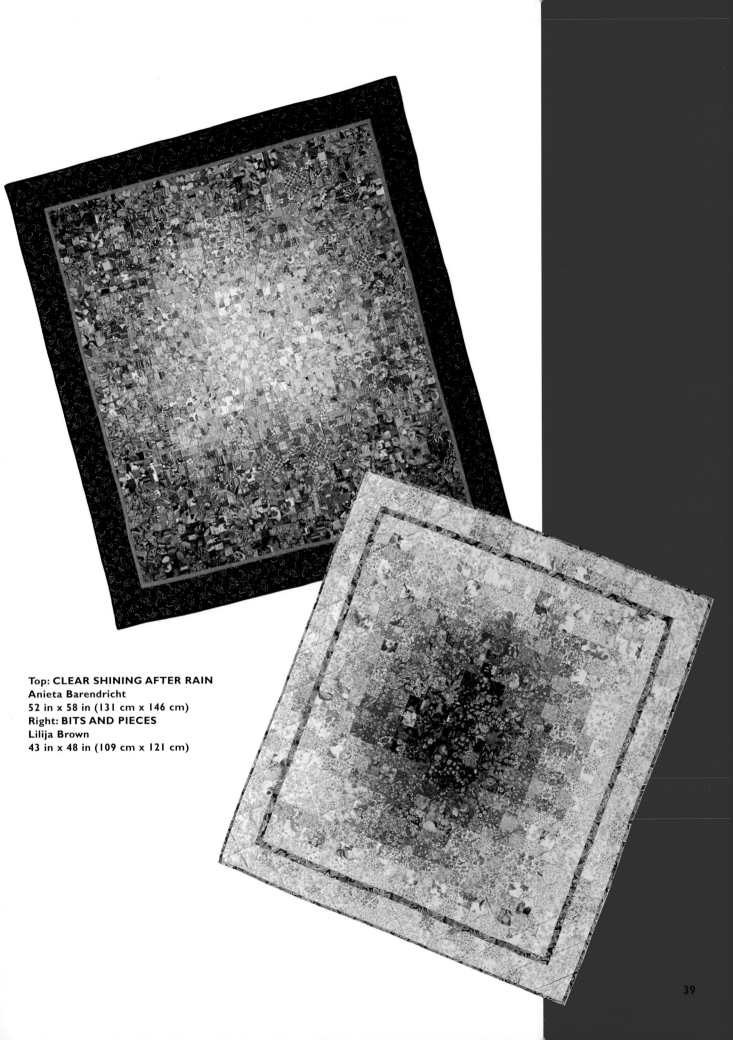

Top: **CLEAR SHINING AFTER RAIN**
Anieta Barendricht
52 in x 58 in (131 cm x 146 cm)
Right: **BITS AND PIECES**
Lilija Brown
43 in x 48 in (109 cm x 121 cm)

If you are shading from corner to corner diagonally, use only half the blocks until you get to the center of the quilt, to make sure you have the other half to complete the quilt top. Complete the quilt by using the left-over blocks.

Stand back and view the quilt while it is hanging. Use value-determining tools to assist you in achieving subtle tonal variation (see page 16) or try squinting. This will help to visually remove the individual fabrics and show where a jump in tonal variation is too great. Move the blocks around to achieve the best effect possible.

Joining the blocks

Note: The quilt is joined in four sections for ease of handling.

1 Stack the blocks in rows, beginning at the bottom of the left-hand side. The top left-hand corner block will be on top. Put a pin in this block to mark the top corner of the quilt and leave the pin in place until the quilt is completed. Stack the second row in the same manner, beginning at the bottom. After this, it is safer to remove only one row at a time, just prior to joining it to the other rows.

2 Beginning with the top two blocks from each stack, chain-piece them, using the same seam allowance as before. Little pinning should be necessary – either butt the seams together or stack the seam allowances, lining them up as best you can. Continue joining rows 1 and 2 in this manner. DO NOT CLIP THE THREADS.

3 Open up the sewn blocks and add the blocks from row 3 onto the edge of row 2, in the same order. Join the quilt in four sections. Press the seams between the blocks together in one direction, and with each row of seams running in alternate directions.

Joining the rows

1 Join the rows without clipping the threads. Butt the seams between blocks and line up all the other piecing as you go. Sew slowly and stitch the rows in alternate directions to avoid stretching. When the four sections of the quilt are completed, join them together vertically.

2 Staystitch ⅛ in (3 mm) from the outside edge of the entire quilt.

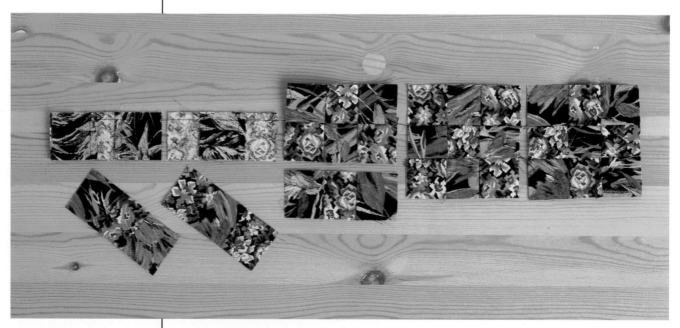

Detail 7: After the second and third sections have been sewn, turn the pile of the first sections over and, beginning where you started, add them to complete the blocks

Borders

1 From the black inner border fabric cut nine strips, 1½ in (4 cm) wide, from selvage to selvage, and join them as required.

2 From the border print fabric, cut down the length of the fabric four strips, 6¼ in (16 cm) wide and 2¾ yd (2.5 m) long.

3 Add the borders following the instructions in the "Adding Borders" section in Technical Details on page 13.

Quilting

To blend color, it is necessary to cross over piecing lines. This can be done by quilting diagonally from corner to corner through the center of the blocks in a straight line or with a gentle, wiggly line. Stitch diagonally through each block in both directions. Use a chalk wheel to extend the line for quilting through the borders.

TO FINISH
Binding

1 Cut nine strips, 2½ in (6 cm) wide on the straight grain. Join them as required to achieve the desired length.

2 Add the binding, following the instructions in the "Binding" section in Technical Details on page 14.

Top: **STRESS RELEASE**
Marcia Jackson
42 in x 44 in (105 cm x 110 cm)
Right: COLORWASH NINE-PATCH
Sandy Lew
45 in x 42 in (113 cm x 107 cm)

Reef Wash

YOU WILL NEED

Note: All fabric quantities are calculated on 44 in (112 cm) wide fabric.

- assorted light fabrics for the blocks
- assorted dark fabrics for the blocks
- 1¾ yd (1.6 m) of dark print fabric for the seam-covering strips and binding
- 3 yd (2.8 m) of fabric for the backing
- 5½ yd (4.6 m) of thin, firm batting, 29 in (74 cm) wide
- sewing machine
- rotary cutter, mat, and ruler
- thread to blend with the fabrics
- thread to match the backing fabric
- large and small square rulers
- long glass-headed pins

Finished size: 42 in × 63 in (105 cm × 157.5 cm)
Finished size of the blocks: 5 in (12.5 cm)
Diagonal measurement of the finished blocks: 7 in (17.5 cm)

A recent visit to the Great Barrier Reef inspired my choice of colors for "Reef Wash." The light fabrics are reminiscent of the clear water and the darker fabrics of the flashes of brilliant coral and the fish that inhabit the Reef.

As well as light and dark fabrics, medium-tone fabrics have been used as either light or dark blocks to vary the coloring of the quilt.

The quilt-as-you-go blocks have been joined by machine-sewing, and the seams are covered with strips of fabric on the back, creating a grid. If you wish to avoid the bulk created by joining the quilt this way, construct the blocks in the same manner, securing them onto batting but eliminating the backing. Back the entire quilt after blocks are joined, then tie the top through to the back of the quilt.

Note: The instructions are for a lap quilt. If you wish to make a larger quilt, for example 84 in × 98 in (210 cm × 245 cm), you would need a total of 310 squares and twenty-six larger squares for the triangle blocks, set on point.

INSTRUCTIONS
Cutting

1. From the light and dark fabrics, cut a selection of strips, varying in width from 1–2 in (2.5–5 cm).
2. From the backing fabric, cut from selvage to selvage:
   - fourteen strips, 6¼ in (16 cm) wide, cross-cut into ninety-four 6¼ in (16 cm) squares for the square blocks;
   - two strips, 6¾ in (17 cm) wide, cross-cut until you have twelve 6¾ in (17 cm) squares for the triangle blocks; cut one extra square of this size from the remaining fabric for a total of thirteen squares;
   - one only 7 in (18 cm) square for the four corner triangles.

Detail 1: Position the first strip diagonally across the batting

Detail 2: Position the second strip on top of the first and stitch through all layers

REEF WASH
Judy Turner

3 From the batting cut:
- twenty-four strips, 6¼ in (16 cm) wide, cross-cut until you have ninety-four 6¼ in (16 cm) squares;
- three strips, 6¾ in (17 cm) wide, cross-cut until you have twelve 6¾ in (17 cm) squares for the triangle blocks;
- cut one extra 6¾ in (17 cm) square for a total of thirteen squares;
- one only 7 in (18 cm) square for the corner triangles.

4 On the lengthwise grain of the seam-covering/binding fabric cut:
- two strips, 3 in × 63 in (7.5 cm × 160 cm) for the binding;
- two strips, 3 in × 44 in (7.5 cm × 109 cm) for the binding;
- ten strips, 1¼ in × 63 in (3.5 cm × 160 cm) for the seam-covering strips on the back of the quilt.

Making the blocks
Note: Use ¼ in (7.5 mm) seam allowances.
For the square blocks
1 Pin the 6¼ in (16 cm) squares of batting to the same size squares of backing, with the pins on the batting side and the wrong side of the fabric facing the batting.

2 Position the first strip diagonally across the batting (detail 1).

3 Position the second strip on top of the first strip, with the right sides together and the seam down the right-hand side (detail 2). Make sure the strip is long enough to cover the batting when the top strip is turned back (detail 3). Finger press.

4 Continue adding strips in this same manner, until one side of the square is covered with strips, then turn the square and continue adding strips in the same manner until the square is completely covered (detail 4).

5 Cover forty squares with dark fabric and fifty-four squares with light fabric. It is important to blend the colors as you add the strips, so there is not too much contrast between strips which are side by side. Cut more strips of varying widths, as you need them.

6 Trim each block by first turning it over and cutting away to the edge of backing fabric (detail 5), then trim each block to a 5½ in (14 cm) square, using a square ruler. Make sure the diagonal line on the ruler is parallel with the seams.

For the triangle blocks
1 Pin the 6¾ in (17 cm) squares of backing to the same size batting squares.

2 Cover all thirteen squares with dark

Detail 3: The strips must be long enough to cover the batting when turned back

Detail 4: Continue adding strips until the square of batting is completely covered

fabric in the same manner as the light fabric squares. Trim each square to 6 in (15 cm).

3   Cut five squares in half through the center horizontally and parallel to the strips for the top and bottom of the quilt (detail 6).

4   Cut eight squares in half through the center vertically for the sides of the quilt (detail 7).

5   For the corner triangles, pin a 7 in (18 cm) square of backing to the same-sized piece of the batting. Cover this square with dark fabrics as in steps 2–5

above. Trim the square back to 6¼ in (16 cm), then cut it through the center diagonally in both directions (detail 8).

Constructing the quilt

Note: All the strips run horizontally across the quilt.

1   Arrange the blocks as shown in the photograph, on the vertical work surface.

2   The long seam-covering strips can be measured as you go, leaving the remainder for short pieces, which will be cut as required. Beginning at the top left-hand corner, join the dark triangle to

Detail 5: Trim the block to the edge of the backing, then to a 5½ in (14 cm) square

Detail 6: Cut five squares in half horizontally for the top and bottom of the quilt

Detail 7: Cut eight squares in half vertically for the sides of the quilt

Detail 8: Trim the square back to 6¼ in (16 cm), then cut it into quarters, as shown

Above: The seam-covering strips form a grid on the back of the quilt

(7.5 mm) seam allowance.

4   Grade the seam allowances, trimming back as much as possible to reduce bulk.

5   Fold the strip so the seam is covered, turn under the raw edge and blindstitch it in place by hand. The finished width must be consistent throughout the quilt. It is important to always sew the seam-covering strips on the same side when joining, so that the grid formed on the back will line up when all the diagonal rows are joined together.

6   Repeat this process until the quilt is joined into diagonal rows. The top left-hand and bottom right-hand corners can be added last.

7   Pin the first and second diagonal rows together with the length of seam-covering strip in place, as you did before. Make sure that the squares line up by pinning at the joins. Trim the seam allowances to reduce bulk, particularly where the blocks meet. Turn the seam-covering strip to cover the seam. Turn under the raw edge and blindstitch as before.

8   Join the whole quilt top in diagonal rows.

TO FINISH
Binding
Add the previously cut binding strips following the instructions in the "Binding" section in Technical Details on page 14.

either side of the light square. Place the right side of the triangle on top of the right side of the square, aligning and pinning a seam-covering strip on top, right side down (details 9 and 10). I have used the wrong side of the fabric as the right side, in this instance, as the right side of the fabric was too dark.

3   Stitch through all layers, using a ¼ in

Details 9 and 10: Join a dark triangle to opposite sides of a light square, aligning and pinning a seam-covering strip on top, right side down

Outback Safari

Finished size: 62 in × 87 in
(155 cm × 221.5 cm)

The initial idea for the design of this quilt came from a black and white sketch of a floor rug. The print fabrics are busy, varied, and they all work with the striped fabric I chose for the quilt. This is a simple quilt using the striped fabric and the subtle contrast to pull the colors together.

INSTRUCTIONS
Cutting
1   From the assorted prints, cut strips of random widths between 1¼–2½ in (3.5–6 cm), from selvage to selvage. I cut two strips from each of my fifty-two fabrics.
2   From the striped fabric, cut from selvage to selvage:
    • three strips, 4½ in (11.5 cm) wide;
    • thirty strips, 1¼ in (3.5 cm) wide.
3   From the gold inner border fabric, cut six

strips 2½ in (6 cm) wide. Join two pairs of these strips for long sides of the quilt.

Making the quilt center
Note: See page 12 for tips on sewing strips.
1   Sew the strips from light to dark in four sections. Each section must be 14¼ in × 41 in (36.5 cm × 104 cm). Sew the rows in alternate directions to avoid stretching the fabric.
2   Sew 4½ in × 41 in (11.5 cm × 104 cm) strips of striped fabric between the four sections to join them and complete the center of the quilt.
3   Sew the gold inner border first to the top and bottom of the quilt, then to the sides of the quilt.

For the border blocks
1   From the darkest fabrics, sew two sections the width of the fabric, at least 7¾ in × 44 in (19.5 × 112 cm) wide.
2   Repeat with the lightest fabrics.

YOU WILL NEED
Note: All fabric quantities are calculated on 44 in (112 cm) wide fabric.
■   assorted light, medium, and dark fabrics – I used fifty-two different prints
■   1⅔ yd (1.5 m) of striped fabric
■   1 yd (90 cm) of gold fabric for the inner border and binding
■   5 yd (4.6 m) of fabric for the backing
■   66 in x 91 in (165 cm x 230 cm) of batting
■   sewing machine
■   rotary cutter, mat, and ruler
■   thread to blend with the fabrics
■   thread to match the backing fabric
■   large square ruler
■   chalk wheel
■   safety pins

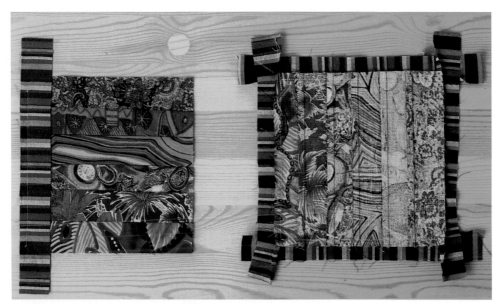

Detail 1 (Left): Stitch a strip of striped fabric along one edge
Detail 2 (Right): Repeat for the other three sides, ensuring the stitching lines meet at the corners

**Right: The effect
of mitered
corners in the
striped fabric is
quite dramatic**

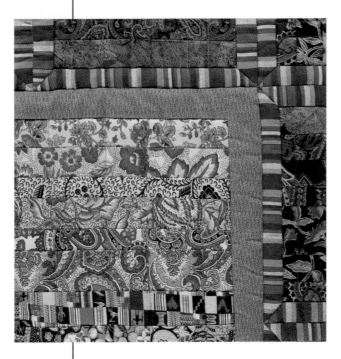

From the remaining fabric

1 Sew the fabric from light to dark in six
   sections that measure a minimum 7¾ in
   × 15½ in (19.5 cm × 39 cm).
2 Cut two 7¾ in (19.5 cm) squares from
   each of the six sewn sections. A total of
   thirty border blocks is needed.
3 For framing the border blocks, cut the
   thirty strips 1¼ in (3.5 cm) wide into
   four equal lengths.
4 Center the striped fabric along one edge
   of a block, with the right sides together,
   and stitch from the wrong side of the
   pieced fabric to within ¼ in (7.5 mm) of
   each end of the block (detail 1). Back-
   track at the beginning and at the end.
   Open out the fabric and repeat on the
   remaining three sides. The stitching lines
   must meet at the corners (detail 2).
5 Mark an angle of 45 degrees from the
   point where the stitching meets to the
   outside edge of the block, using a ruler
   with a 45-degree angle or a 45-degree
   set square, and mark the stitching line on
   the wrong side with a chalk wheel
   (detail 3). This method gives a very

3. Cut the sewn fabric into 7¾ in (19.5 cm)
   squares. You will need nine dark and nine
   light squares. To do this, cut the fabric
   into 7¾ in (19.5 cm) sections, and trim
   back the top and bottom to make a
   square.

**Detail 3: Mark an angle of 45 degrees from the point where
the stitching meets to the outside edge of the block**

**Detail 4: Trim the excess fabric, leaving a ¼ in (7.5 mm) seam
allowance and press the seam open**

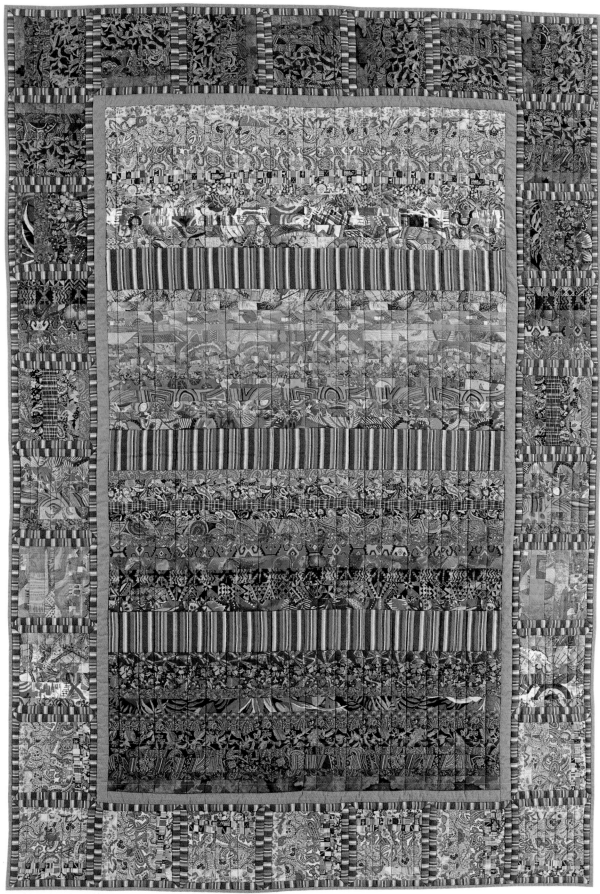

OUTBACK SAFARI
Judy Turner

accurate miter. Mark each end of the striped fabric in this way.

6 Pin the adjacent borders, matching the chalk lines, and stitch, back-tracking at the beginning of the seam. Trim the excess fabric, leaving a ¼ in (7.5 mm) seam allowance and press the seam open (detail 4).

7 If you prefer not to miter the corners, join the striped fabric to the edges of every block by sewing two opposite sides, then the other two (detail 5). The striped fabric is not matched at the corners of each block. This adds a little more interest to the overall quilt design.

Assembling the quilt

1 On the vertical work surface, position the center of the quilt, then arrange the dark blocks around the light end of the quilt, and the light blocks around the dark end. Position the remaining six blocks on either side, gradually blending the color. The border will consist of seven blocks across the width, and ten blocks down the length of the quilt. All blocks have the piecing turned in alternate directions.

2 Join the five light blocks, matching where the miters meet. Leave one block on either end as these blocks will form part of the side borders. Repeat with the five dark blocks.

3 Join the ten blocks which form one side border, then repeat with the remaining ten blocks for the other side border.

Constructing the quilt

1 Measure through the center of the quilt and pin-mark the quilt center and the gold borders into quarters. Add a gold inner border to the top and bottom of the quilt. Check your measurements carefully to be sure the outer border will fit, once the inner border is added.

2 Add the gold inner border to both sides of the quilt. This inner border has been cut a little wider than needed, so you can adjust the center measurement of the quilt to fit the pieced borders. Trim, so the outer borders will fit.

3 Add the outer border of five joined blocks to the top and bottom.

4 Add the outer border of ten joined border blocks to both sides of the quilt.

5 Layer the completed quilt top with batting and backing in preparation for machine-quilting.

Quilting
Note: See page 13 for "Preparation for Machine-Quilting."
Quilt as desired, using a chalk wheel to mark any necessary lines.

TO FINISH
Binding

1 Cut seven strips, 2½ in (6 cm) wide of gold fabric, from selvage to selvage. Join the strips as required.

2 Add the binding, following the instructions in the "Binding" section in Technical Details on page 14.

Detail 5: If you prefer not to miter the corners, join the striped fabric to opposite sides of the block, then to the other two sides

Spring

Finished size: 106 in (270 cm) square
Finished blocks size: 8½ in (21.5 cm) square
Diagonal measurement of finished block: 12 in × 12 in (30 cm × 30 cm)

I gathered these fabrics as their colors remind me of spring with its blossoms, flowers, and clear days. While very dark fabrics have been eliminated, there is still a great difference in value between the lightest and darkest fabrics used.

Note: A zigzag stitch on your machine is essential for the construction of this quilt.

INSTRUCTIONS

Before you begin cutting, arrange the fabrics from light to dark. Begin cutting the light fabrics first.

Cutting

1 From the assorted print fabrics, cut strips from selvage to selvage in varying widths from 1¼–2 in (3.5–5 cm).
2 Arrange the cut strips from light to dark; extra strips will be cut as required.
3 From the backing fabric, cut forty-one 9 ½ in (24 cm) wide strips, from selvage to selvage. Cross-cut them into 163 squares 9½ in (24 cm).
4 From the batting, cut fifty-five strips, 9½ in × 29 in (24 cm × 74 cm). Cross-cut them into 163 squares 9½ in (24 cm).
5 From the seam-covering/binding fabric, cut ten strips 3¾ in (9.5 cm) wide from selvage to selvage, for the binding.
6 Cut 131 strips 1¼ in (3.5 cm) wide from selvage to selvage, for the seam-covering strips (front and back). Cross-cut sixty-four of these strips into 8½ in (21.5 cm) sections – a total of 320 short strips.

Making the blocks

Note: Use ¼ in (7.5 mm) seam allowances.

1 Pin the 9½ in (24 cm) squares of backing fabric to the same size squares of batting. Pin on the batting side with the wrong side of the backing fabric facing the batting.
2 Beginning in the center of the quilt with the lightest strips, position the first strip on the extreme left-hand side of the batting, vertically and with the right side facing up.

YOU WILL NEED

Note: All fabric quantities are calculated on 44 in (112 cm) wide fabric.

- assorted light, medium, and dark print fabrics
- 11 yd (10 m) of firm cotton fabric for the backing
- 6 yd (5.6 m) of floral print fabric for the seam-covering strips (front and back) and the binding
- 14½ yd (13.2 m) of thin, firm batting, 29 in (74 cm) wide
- sewing machine
- rotary cutter, mat, and ruler
- thread to blend with the fabrics
- thread to match the backing fabric
- large square ruler
- long glass-headed pins

Detail 1: With the second strip on top of the first, stitch down the right side

Detail 2: Finger-press the strip towards the batting and add the rest of the strips

Detail 3: Trim the blocks, then staystitch the outside edge

Right: The blocks are placed so the strips are running in alternate directions

3 Position the second strip on top of the first strip, with the right sides together. Stitch through all layers down the right-hand edge (detail 1).

4 Finger-press the second strip towards the batting so the right side of the fabric is facing. Add subsequent strips in the same way (detail 2), and continue adding strips until the square is totally covered.

5 Make 145 blocks altogether, with the blocks gradually becoming darker. The remaining blocks for the triangle edges of the quilt will be made later.

6 Turn the blocks over and trim the excess fabric to the edge of the batting.

7 Trim the blocks to 8½ in (21.5 cm) squares as you go. Staystitch the outside edges of each block (detail 3).

8 Arrange the blocks on the vertical work surface as you go, with the lightest blocks in the center and with the strips running in alternate directions and the blocks turned on point.

Making the triangles

1 You will need sixteen triangular blocks to fit the outside edges of the quilt. Each one must be tailor-made as far as the depth of color is concerned.

2 The triangles for the top and bottom of the quilt will be made from eight of these blocks in colors that will match the top and bottom of the quilt. Make them in the same way as before, then cut them diagonally through the center to give sixteen triangles (detail 4).

3 The other eight blocks must match the coloring of the side edges of the quilt. Make them in the same way, then cut them diagonally in the opposite direction (detail 5).

4 For the corner triangles, make a block using fabrics which will blend with the colors in the quilt corners. Cut the block into quarters diagonally (detail 6).

Detail 4: Cut eight squares in half as shown for the top and bottom triangles

Detail 5: Cut eight squares in half the other way for the side triangles

Detail 6: For the corner triangles, cut one block into quarters

SPRING
Judy Turner

Note: If any of the corners of the quilt vary in color, you may need to make an extra block or two to enable you to get just the right coloring in each corner. One extra block has been allowed for this possibility.

Constructing the quilt

When all the squares, triangles, and corners are completed and you are happy with the arrangement on the vertical work surface, you are ready to construct the quilt.

1 Join the blocks in diagonal rows, beginning at the top left-hand corner.
2 Pin a 8½ in (21.5 cm) wide strip to both sides of the bottom edge of the top triangle and the center square (detail 7).
3 Using the width of your presser foot, stitch the edge that will butt to the seam-covering strip. This will give you a consistent distance to turn the seam-covering strip to.
4 Join the blocks into diagonal rows by butting the seam allowances together and zigzag stitching, using the widest zigzag stitch. When each diagonal row is completed, turn it over and zigzag again for extra strength.
5 Fold the seam-covering strip, turning the raw edge under until it just meets the previous stitching (detail 8). Blindstitch it in place by hand on the front and the back. The width of this seam must be consistent for the entire quilt.

Joining the diagonal rows

1 Number the rows to avoid confusion, then pin the diagonal rows onto the vertical work surface in the correct order. The remaining seam-covering strips will be joined, as necessary, as the quilt is assembled.
2 Join all the diagonal rows in the same manner as before by stitching seam-covering strips to the right-hand edge of the diagonal rows, front and back. Stitch along the left-hand side of the diagonal rows, the width of your presser foot, as before.
3 Butt the rows of blocks as in step 4. Pin the rows at the junction of the seam-covering strips with two long glass-headed pins (detail 9) and zigzag them together. Continue zigzagging, pinning at each junction as you go. Sew slowly over the pins to avoid breaking the machine needle. Do not forget to turn your work over and zigzag on the back for extra strength.
4 Join the quilt in the above manner into groups of two rows, then groups of four rows, and so on. Hand-finish on the front and back seams as you go (detail 10).
5 The most difficult part in making this quilt is putting the two halves of the quilt together. Sew slowly and carefully and you will have a beautiful, sturdy quilt in the end.

Detail 7 (Top): Pin a strip to both sides of the bottom edge of the top triangle and the center square
Detail 8 (Bottom): Fold the seam-covering strip as shown

Binding

1 Join the ten previously cut 3¾ in (9.5 cm) wide strips so you have four lengths with two-and-a-half strips in each. Line up the binding so it matches the junction of the front seam-covering strips. The finished binding will be twice the width of the seam allowance.

2 Add the binding, following the instructions in the "Binding" section in Technical Details on page 14.

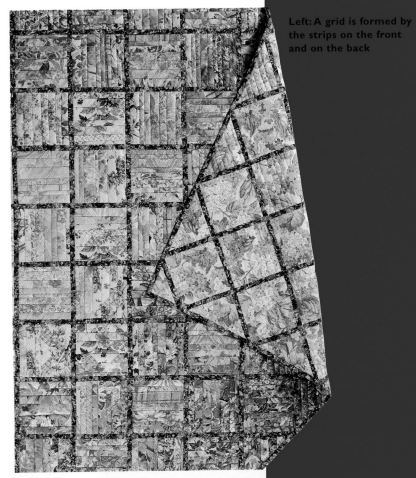

Left: A grid is formed by the strips on the front and on the back

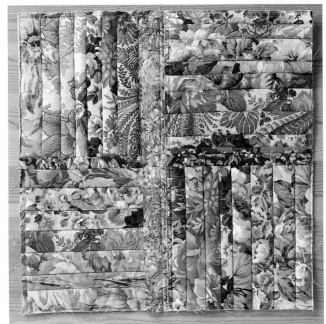

Detail 9: Pin the rows together at the junction of the seam-covering strips, then zigzag them together

Detail 10: Hand-finish on the front and back seam-covering strips as you go

Summer

Note: All fabric quantities are calculated on 44 in (112 cm) wide fabric.

- assorted light, medium, and dark fabrics
- 1½ yd (1.3 m) of blue cotton or chintz fabric for the inserts and binding
- ⅛ yd (10 cm) yellow cotton or chintz fabric for the inserts
- 3⅓ yd (3 m) of fabric for the backing
- 58 in x 85 in (146 cm x 215 cm) of batting
- sewing machine
- rotary cutter, mat, and ruler
- thread to blend with the fabrics
- thread to match the backing fabric
- chalk wheel
- long glass-headed pins
- safety pins

Finished size: 54 in x 80 in (136 cm x 205 cm)

This design has proved to be popular in classes and can be varied a great deal depending on the colors used. Although this quilt has inserts in only two solid colors, many more could be used (see page 59). More than two inserts could also be added in each section, but the number must be consistent for the pieced rows to remain the same length.

INSTRUCTIONS
Cutting
Note: When larger or scattered prints are cut into strips, then cut into 6½ in (16.5 cm) sections, you will find the depth of color can vary greatly within each strip. With this in mind, you may be able to use the same fabric several times in one section.

1 From the assorted prints, cut strips in varying widths from 1¼–2¾ in (3.5–7 cm) from selvage to selvage.

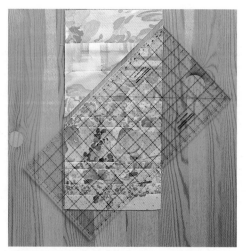

Detail 1: Cut through the pieced fabric you have made at an angle of 45 degrees

2 Cut all the strips into sections 6½ in (16.5 cm) long.

Arranging the quilt
1 Position the first row of sections vertically from dark to light, on the vertical work surface. Move the pieces about, using value-determining tools to guide you.
2 Position the second row of fabric pieces from light to dark, on the vertical work surface. Repeat until you have nine vertical rows, each of which will need to be 80 in (205 cm) long, when joined.

Sewing the sections
Note: Use ¼ in (7.5 mm) seam allowances. Sew the seams in alternate directions. This will help to prevent the sections from stretching out of shape.

1 Sew the sections into groups that are approximately 10 in (25 cm) long. Replace the groups on the vertical work surface as you finish them. By sewing in 10 in (25 cm) groups like this, you will be

Detail 2: Center one insert along the cut edge and stitch it in place

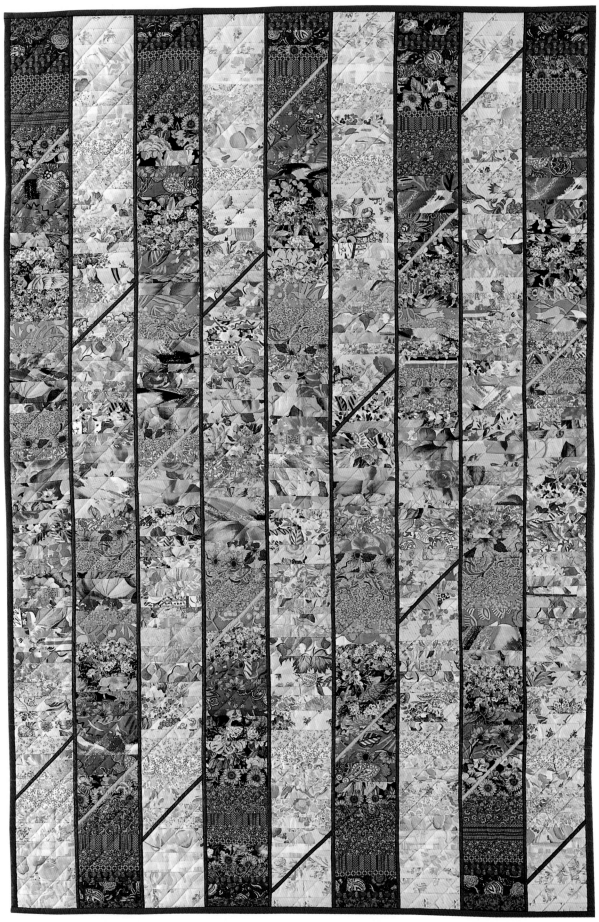

SUMMER
Judy Turner

For the inserts

1 From the blue cotton or chintz fabric cut from selvage to selvage:
 • sixteen strips, 1 in (2.5 cm) wide, which will be joined into groups of two, ready to be used vertically between the nine sections of the quilt;
 • three strips, 1 in (2.5 cm) wide, cut into sections 11 in (28 cm) long which will be used for the diagonal inserts.

2 From the yellow cotton or chintz fabric, cut three 1 in (2.5 cm) wide strips across the width of the fabric, then cut them into 11 in (28 cm) long sections for the diagonal inserts.

3 Decide exactly where to place the diagonal inserts. If you pin the inserts into the vertical rows of piecing, it will help you to distribute the inserts evenly on the quilt surface.

4 To insert diagonal fabric, cut through the pieced fabric at an angle of 45 degrees, at the position you determined previously (detail 1).

5 Center one of the inserts along the cut edge and stitch it in place (detail 2). Press the seam allowances towards the pieced fabric (detail 3).

6 Line up your ruler along the edge of the piecing and trim the excess fabric from the insert so it is in line with the piecing (detail 4).

able to determine whether or not extra sections need to be added. Perhaps some will need to be replaced with wider ones, or the top or bottom cut off to attain the length required. The same fabrics do not need to be used in each row. As long as each is sewn from light to dark, a satisfactory effect will be achieved.

2 When all nine rows have been sewn, make a final adjustment so they are all the same length.

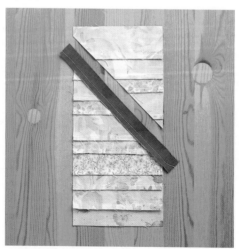

Detail 3: Press the seam allowances towards the pieced fabric

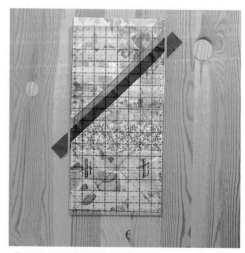

Detail 4: Using the ruler, trim the excess from the insert

7 Center the remaining diagonal edge and sew from vertex to vertex (i.e. from the junction of the fabrics at each end) (detail 5). The horizontal piecing will not line up after the diagonal piece is inserted.

8 Repeat these steps twice within each of the nine vertical sections of the quilt.

Joining the quilt

1 Pin the long narrow blue sections, which are already joined, into position, then sew them between the pieced rows. Make sure your seam allowances are consistent. Press the seam allowances towards the pieced sections (detail 6).

2 Staystitch close to the outside edges of the quilt to prevent stretching.

3 Layer the completed quilt top with batting and backing in preparation for machine-quilting.

Quilting

1 Read the section on "Preparation for Machine-Quilting" on page 13. Quilt in-the-ditch, on either side of the long vertical inserts.

2 Quilt the diagonal inserts in the same way.

3 Mark the quilt top in diagonal lines, using the chalk wheel. Quilt along these lines.

4 When the quilting is completed, trim, leaving extra backing and batting to fill the wider-than-usual binding.

TO FINISH
Binding

1 From the blue cotton or chintz fabric, cut seven strips 4¼ in (11 cm) wide from selvage to selvage. Join them as required for the binding.

2 Add the binding, following the instructions in Technical Details on page 14.

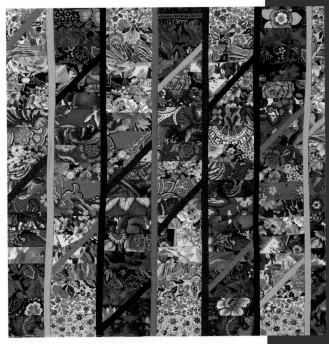

Left: A change in color creates a dramatic difference

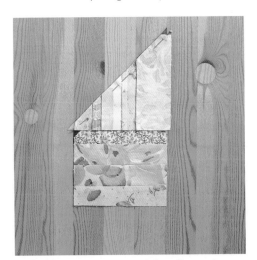

Detail 5: Center the remaining diagonal edge and sew from vertex to vertex

Detail 6: Sew the long narrow blue sections into place between the pieced rows

Colorwash Cascade

YOU WILL NEED

Note: All fabric quantities are calculated on 44 in (112 cm) wide fabric.

- assorted light, medium, and dark prints (I have used approximately 200 different fabrics)
- 2⅞ yd (2.6 m) of dark print fabric for the outer border and binding
- 18 in (50 cm) of a medium print fabric for the inner border
- 6⅔ yd (6 m) of fabric for the backing
- 84 in x 120 in (2.1 m x 3 m) of batting
- sewing machine
- rotary cutter, mat, and ruler
- thread to blend with the fabrics
- thread to match the backing fabric
- small square ruler
- safety pins

Finished size: 80 in x 116 in (199.5 cm x 289.5 cm)

A combination of bold and subtle contrast creates a feeling of cascading color in this quilt which uses both Nine-patch and Rail-fence blocks in a large variety of busy prints. The inner border seems to disappear and reappear, because it is the same value as some of the fabrics at the edge of the quilt.

INSTRUCTIONS
Cutting the Rail-fence blocks

Cut one strip 1½ in (4 cm) wide from each of the assorted print fabrics, cut from selvage to selvage. Make sure you have a large section of fabrics, from light to dark.

Arranging the fabrics

Line up the strips from light to dark so you can see only a small amount of each fabric. Using one of the value determining tools (see page 16), check that the colors are blending and in the correct position. Shift any fabrics that are in the wrong position and eliminate any that stand out and do not blend with those around it.

Making the Rail-fence blocks

Note: Use ¼ in (7.5 mm) seam allowances and a smaller than usual stitch.

1 Sew the strips in groups of three, from dark to light, making sure you sew in alternate directions to avoid stretching. Be consistent with your seam allowance at all times. You will achieve a greater variety of pieced squares if all the strips are not the same length. Cut a section off the first strip (detail 1). If your fabrics are all the same length, cut a section off a few more strips in the same way. Always join the strips from light to dark, using up every bit of fabric that is at least as long as the width of your three sewn strips to achieve as many combinations of fabrics as possible, while at the same time always joining from light to dark (detail 2).

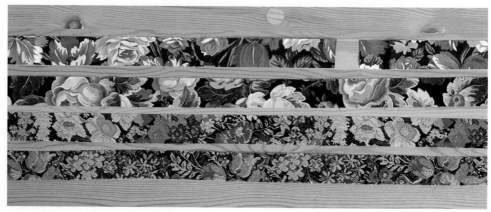

Detail 1: To achieve a greater variety, cut a section off the first strip

COLORWASH CASCADE
Judy Turner

Right: A detail of
"Colorwash Cascade"
showing the Nine-
patch piecing

2 Press the seams together in one
   direction.
3 Check the width of your sewn groups of
   three strips. Cut squares this size from all
   the groups of strips (detail 3). The blocks
   should be 3½ in (9 cm) square. You will
   need a total of 624 Rail-fence blocks.

For the Nine-patch blocks

Note: If you prefer, replace the Nine-patch
block insert at the top of the quilt with Rail-
fence blocks, in which case you will need
another eighty Rail-fence blocks.

Cutting

Select sixty-four different fabrics which blend
in color from light to dark. Cut one 1¼ in
(3.5 cm) wide strip from selvage to selvage
from each of the sixty-four fabrics.

Arranging the strips

1 Arrange the strips from light to dark
   with the same amount of each fabric
   showing. Shift the position of strips until
   you have a flow of color from light to
   dark.
2 Arrange the fabric into pairs; beginning at
   the light end, start pairing fabrics by
   moving up the range of values only as far
   as you need to. Within each pair, the
   fabrics only need to be of a different
   scale, or one fabric should be just slightly
   darker than the other. Mix the colors as
   you are putting them in pairs. If you
   move from the light strips gradually to
   the dark strips, you will have
   automatically paired: light with light, light
   with medium, medium with medium,
   medium with dark and dark with dark.
3 Place the pairs together with the right
   sides facing. Fold them into three equal
   lengths, then cut them at the folds. You
   will have three identical pairs of strips,
   with the right sides together.

Sewing the strips

You will need to take a slightly larger seam
allowance for the Nine-patch insert. The
blocks should be approximately 2 in (5 cm)
finished size, or 2½ in (6.5 cm) including
seam allowances. This will enable the Nine-
patch insert to fit in with the Rail-fence
piecing. Use a slightly smaller stitch than
usual, as there will be no back-tracking.

**Detail 2: Always join the strips from light to dark, using up every bit of
fabric that is at least as long as the width of the sewn strips**

1 Work with one set at a time, making sure the strips are the same length, before you begin sewing. Sew two different strips together with the right sides facing.

2 Without clipping the thread, sew the next two, making sure that the different fabric is on top (detail 4).

3 Add the third strip to the last pair you have sewn, then to the other pair. (This way, the strips will have been sewn in alternate directions.) You will have two lots of three strips with the colors in alternate positions (detail 5). Press the seam allowances together in alternate directions within each set. Leave them flat, with right sides together, until you are ready to cut them.

Cutting the sets

On your cutting mat, line up as many single sets as the size of the mat allows. Have them with the right sides together and the left-hand end of the sets in line. Square up the left-hand side of the group of strips, then cut into 1¼ in (3.5 cm) sections. Stack the sections in groups of three as you go, without flipping them over, making sure every second set is turned so the right side is facing (detail 6). By stacking them in a crisscross fashion, you will alternate the color arrangements. Three sections will make a block, and there will be two different blocks from the same fabrics (detail 7).

Left: A detail of "Colorwash Cascade" showing the Rail-fence piecing

Sewing the blocks

1 Lift the first group of three from the stack. Place the first section right side down beside your machine. Chain-piece the other two sections together, butting the seam allowances. Without clipping the threads, and again placing the first section face down beside the machine, sew the next two sections together.

2 Continue in this manner until the first two sections of the whole set have been sewn, then turn the pile of first sections over and add them, one section at a time, beginning where you started (detail 8). You will need 180 blocks. Press the seams together in any direction. Each pair of strips will yield six blocks, giving you a total of 192 blocks – fifteen blocks across and twelve blocks down.

Detail 3: Cut squares the same size as the width of the sewn sections from all the groups of strips

Chain-piecing the Nine-patch insert

The Nine-patch insert can be chain-pieced, ready to be inserted into the rest of the quilt. Stack the blocks in rows, beginning at the bottom of the left-hand side; the top left-hand corner block will be on top. Put a pin in this block to mark the top corner of the quilt and leave the pin in place until the quilt is completed. Stack the second row in this manner, beginning at the bottom. After this it is safer to remove only one row at a time, just prior to joining it to the other rows.

1   Begin with the top two blocks from each stack and chain-piece them, using the same seam allowance as before. Little pinning should be necessary; either butt the seams together or stack the seam allowances. Continue joining rows 1 and 2 in this manner. DO NOT CLIP THE THREADS.

2   Open up the sewn blocks and add the blocks from row 3 to the edge of row 2, in the same order. After all the blocks are joined in vertical rows, the quilt should be held together by the thread between the rows of blocks.

3   Press the seams between the blocks together in one direction, with each row of seams running in alternate directions.

Joining the rows

Join the rows, without clipping the threads, by butting the seams between blocks and lining up all other piecing as you go. Sew slowly and stitch the rows in alternate directions to avoid stretching the fabric. When the Nine-patch section is completed you are ready to assemble the quilt.

Note: If you are using all Rail-fence blocks, there is no need to join the insert, before the remainder of the quilt is assembled.

Arranging the Rail-fence blocks

1   Beginning at the bottom of the quilt, arrange the blocks on the vertical work surface. Position the blocks so the strips are running in alternate directions (vertical and horizontal). None of the strips will line up when joined. The quilt is twenty-two Rail-fence blocks wide and thirty-four Rail-fence blocks long. There are six Rail-fence blocks between the inserts and the borders. Refer to the quilt photograph for a guide to color placement.

2   Chain-piece the quilt into five horizontal sections. When adding the Nine-patch section, you may have to adjust seams slightly for it to fit.

3   Staystitch ⅛ in (3 mm) from the outside edge of the entire quilt.

Detail 4 (Top): Sew two strips together, then the next two, making sure a different fabric is on top
Detail 5 (Bottom): You will have two lots of three strips, as shown

Borders

1   From the inner border fabric, cut nine 1¾ in (4.5 cm) strips, from selvage to selvage. Join them as required to achieve the desired length.

2   From the dark border print, cut four strips, 6 in × 103 in (15 cm × 2.6 m), down the length of the fabric for the outer border, and four strips, 2½ in × 103 in (6 cm × 2.6 m), for the binding.

3   Add the borders, following the instructions in the "Adding Borders" section in Technical Details on page 13.

4   Layer the completed quilt top with the batting and backing in preparation for machine-quilting.

Quilting

To quilt with a diagonal grid, draw lines with the chalk wheel from corner to corner, diagonally through the Rail-fence blocks. Mark only a few lines at a time as the chalk will wear off. If you have inserted a Nine-patch section, ignore the piecing and draw a chalk line through this patch from the center of the Rail-fence blocks on one side of the quilt through to the other side.

TO FINISH
Binding

Join the previously cut 2½ in × 103 in (6 cm × 2.6 m) binding strips as required. Add the binding following the instructions in the "Binding" section in Technical Details on page 14.

Detail 6 (Left): Stack the section in groups of three, as shown
Detail 7 (Middle): The same fabrics will yield two blocks
Detail 8 (Right): Add the first sections to the previously sewn pair

Black Jewel

Note: All fabric quantities are calculated on 44 in (112 cm) wide fabric.

- ⅛ yd (10 cm) each of ninety-six different printed fabrics
- 4⅞ yd (4.4 m) of black cotton fabric
- 2¾ yd (2.5 m) of multicolored print fabric for the triangles and binding
- 7⅔ yd (7 m) of fabric for the backing
- 95 in x 103 in (230 cm x 260 cm) of batting
- sewing machine
- rotary cutter, mat, and ruler
- thread to blend with the fabrics
- thread to match the backing fabric
- small square ruler
- safety pins
- chalk wheel

Finished size: 90½ in × 99 in (221.5 cm × 251.5 cm)

I came across this design while experimenting with different ideas for one of my classes. The shading in "Black Jewel" is achieved by piecing sashing strips in a gentle gradation from light to dark. The multicolored print featured in the large triangles was the starting point for all the other fabrics I chose for this quilt.

INSTRUCTIONS

Cutting and sewing the sashing strips

Note: Use ¼ in (7.5 mm) seam allowances and a smaller than usual stitch.

1 From selvage to selvage cut two strips 1½ in (4 cm) wide from each of the ninety-six printed fabrics.
2 Arrange the printed strips from light to dark so the same amount of each fabric is showing. Make sure you have a flow of color before you begin sewing (see "Color Value" on page 9).

3 Sew the strips from light to dark in groups of four (detail 1), making sure you sew the rows in alternate directions to avoid stretching the fabrics. You should have twenty-three different groups of four sewn strips. Press the seams together in one direction, towards the darker fabric.
4 Cut the sewn strips into 2½ in (6 cm) sections (detail 2). Each sewn unit should yield seventeen sections.
5 Only three extra 2½ in (6 cm) wide sections are needed of each group of four sewn strips. Sew them in the same order by either cutting an 8 in (20 cm) section from each strip, or repeat the steps above and use the leftover pieced fabric in another quilt (see page 69).

Large half-square triangles

1 The length of the four sewn strips (detail 3) will determine the size of the half-square triangles. Measure several of your sashing sections to determine this size. If some are a little longer, either trim them

Detail 1 (Top): Sew the strips from light to dark in groups of four
Detail 2 (Bottom): Cut the sewn strips into sections

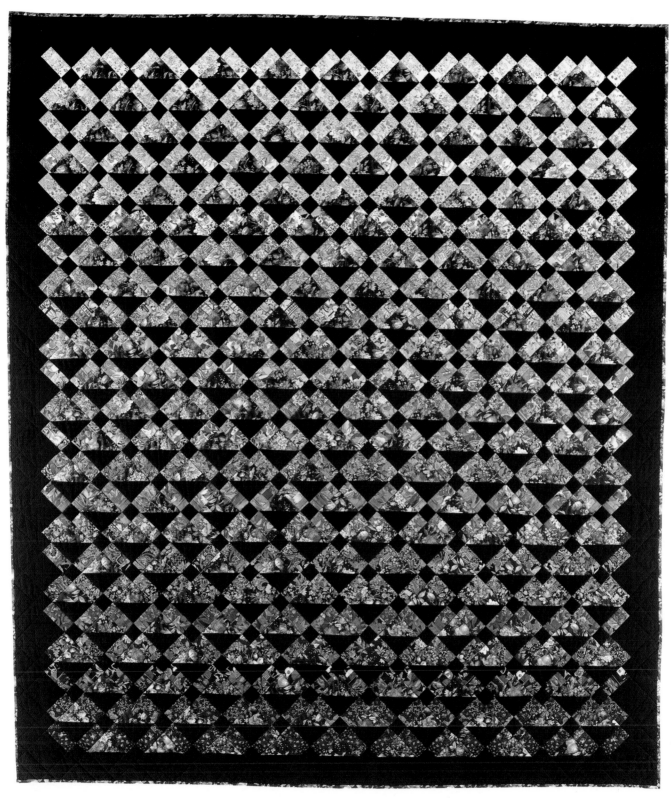

BLACK JEWEL
Judy Turner

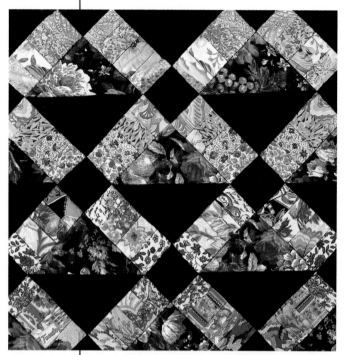

2.5 cm = 12.5 cm). This measurement will determine the size of the half-square triangles. It will be referred to as your personal measurement.

2 From the black fabric, cut fourteen strips from selvage to selvage the width of your personal measurement. Cross-cut the strips until you have 105 squares. Cut these squares in half diagonally. You will need 209 black triangles.

3 From the multicolored print cut six strips down the length of the fabric, the width of your personal measurement and 99 in (2.5 m) long. Cross-cut these strips until you have 105 squares. Cut these squares in half diagonally. You will need 209 print triangles. Cut a further ten triangles the same size, with the straight grain on the longest side, for the bottom of the quilt, and set them aside.

4 Sew the black triangles to the print triangles, with the right sides together. These can be chain-pieced, then snipped apart (detail 4). Press the seams together, towards the dark fabric.

back or adjust your sewing. The sections should be approximately 4½ in (11.5 cm), including seam allowances on the ends, so the finished size should be approximately 4 in (10 cm). To the finished size, add ⅞ in (2.5 cm), for example, 4 in + ⅞ in = 4⅞ in (10 cm +

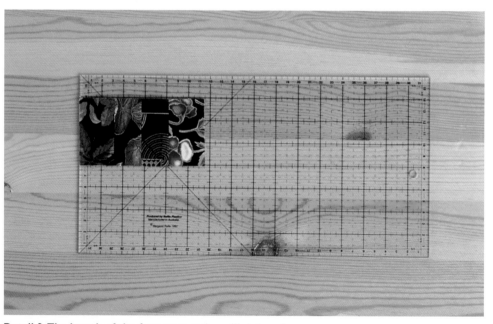

Detail 3: The length of the four sewn strips will determine the size of the half-square triangles

For the border and small squares

From the remaining black fabric, and cutting lengthwise, cut:

• four strips, 4½ in × 103 in (11.5 cm × 2.6 m), for the borders;

• six strips, 2½ in (6 cm) wide, cross-cut until you have 209 squares;

• thirty-two triangles the size of the half-square triangles previously cut, but with the straight grain along the longest edge of triangle; these triangles are for the outside edge on three sides of the quilt;

• thirty-two small triangles with the longest side cut on the straight and the two short sides 2⅞ in (7 cm) long for the outside edge of the quilt;

• two tiny triangles with short sides 2½ in (6 cm) long cut on the straight and the long side on the bias, for the top corners of the quilt;

• one square the size of your personal measurement, cut into quarters, diagonally – two of these triangles are for the bottom corners of the quilt. Take care to cut the short sides of the triangles on the straight grain for the quilt edges.

Above: This quilt is made from the pieces left over from "Black Jewel"

Detail 4: Chain-piece the black triangles to the print triangles, then snip them apart

Arranging the quilt

1 Line up your pieced sashing sections from light to dark before you begin, so you will have them in the correct order. On the vertical work surface, arrange all the pieces using the photograph as a guide. All twenty identical sashing sections will run across the quilt, with the lightest part of each section to the top and the darkest to the bottom (detail 5). Position all the sashing sections first, from light at the top of the quilt to dark at the bottom of the quilt.

2 Fill in with small dark squares turned on-point and pieced squares turned on-point with the point section to the top.

3 At the bottom of the quilt, fill in with the large print triangles with the outside edge cut on the straight grain. At the top and on both sides, fill in with the large black triangles with the outside edges cut on the straight grain.

4 Fill around the outside edges of the quilt with the remaining small triangles and the tiny triangles at the top corners and the remaining triangles at the bottom corners (detail 6).

Constructing the quilt

1 Join the quilt in diagonal rows, beginning at the top left-hand corner, or chain-piece in the following manner: stack the sections from left-hand side in diagonal rows; after the first two rows are joined, take another row off the work surface and add one piece at a time to the first two rows. Do not snip thread. The outside triangles can only be added as the next row is sewn.

2 Continue this process until you have joined one-quarter of the quilt in one direction. Press the seams towards the darker fabric.

3 Join the rows together by flipping one row at a time and sewing with the right sides together and butting the seam allowances as you go. Sew the rows in alternate directions.

4 When one-quarter of the quilt is completed, join the next quarter in the same manner, and so on. The quilt is divided into four just to make it easier to manage the bulk.

5 When all four sections of the quilt are completed, staystitch close to the outside edge, on all sides, to prevent stretching.

Detail 5: All twenty identical sashing sections run across the quilt with the lightest area at the top

Borders

Add the four 4½ in (11.5 cm) wide previously cut black strips to the quilt, following the "Adding Borders" instructions in the section in Technical Details on page 13.

Quilting

1 Layer the completed quilt top with batting and backing in preparation for machine-quilting.
2 Read "Preparation for Machine-Quilting" on page 13. Quilt diagonally, in-the-ditch, down either side of the sashing sections in both directions.
3 If you wish, quilt in-the-ditch between the large print and the black triangles, starting and stopping inside the square.

Binding

1 From the multicolored print fabric, cut four strips, 2½ in × 99 in (6 cm × 2.5 m), lengthwise, joining them if necessary.
2 Add the binding following the instructions in the "Binding" section in Technical Details on page 14.

Detail 6: Fill in around the edges of the quilt with the remaining small triangles (this is a sample)

Winter Surprise

Finished size: 68½ in x 90½ in
(174 cm x 229 cm)

Beautiful flowers, such as camellias and
daisies, are always a welcome surprise during
the winter months. The large floral print
fabric was a starting point for the collection
of multicolored plaids, reflecting the blue,
pink, and ocher coloring of the flowers.
Plaids and checks are rarely printed on the
straight grain, so ignore the direction of the
printed lines and cut the strips perfectly
straight. The variations of line will add
interest to the quilt.

INSTRUCTIONS
Cutting

1   Cut the light and dark plaids into 2½ in
    (6 cm) wide strips from selvage to
    selvage. Cut the length of the strips in
    half so you can vary the combinations
    more readily.
2   From the border/binding fabric, cut
    down the length of the fabric: four 6½ in
    (16.5 cm) wide strips for the borders,
    and four 2½ in (6 cm) wide strips for the
    binding. Cut some of the remaining fabric

into 2½ in (6 cm) wide strips for piecing
the dark blocks.

Sewing the Four-patch blocks
Note: Use ¼ in (7.5 mm) seam allowances
and a smaller than usual stitch.

1   You will need 120 light Four-patch blocks
    altogether. Beginning with the light strips,
    join the half strips into pairs, in many
    different combinations (details 1a and 1b).
    Press the seams together in one direction.
2   Cut the sewn strips into 2½ in (6 cm)
    wide sections (detail 2).
3   Join sections from one sewn unit with
    sections from another sewn unit (detail
    3). Butt the seam allowances in alternate
    directions. Press the seams together in
    one direction.
4   Repeat this process with the dark fabrics
    and make 254 dark Four-patch blocks.

Arranging the blocks

1   Beginning in the center of the vertical
    work surface, arrange the dark blocks in
    a rectangle that is eight blocks high and
    seven blocks wide.
2   Surround the center rectangle with light

**Detail 1a: Join the light strips into pairs in
many different combinations**

**Detail 1b: Pair up combinations of dark
plaid fabrics as for the light plaid fabrics**

WINTER SURPRISE
Judy Turner

blocks that are two rows deep at the sides and four rows deep at the top and bottom.

3   Using the remaining dark blocks, add three more rows of blocks around each side of the light blocks. The quilt should be twenty-two blocks long and seventeen blocks wide.

Constructing the quilt

Note: The quilt is joined in four sections for ease of handling.

1   Stack the blocks in rows, beginning at the bottom of the left-hand side. The top left-hand corner block will be on top. Put a pin in this block to mark the top corner of the quilt and leave the pin in place until the quilt is completed.

2   Stack the second row in the same manner, beginning at the bottom. After this, it is safer to remove only one row at a time from the vertical work surface, just prior to joining it to the other rows.

3   Beginning with the top two blocks from each stack, chain-piece the blocks, using the same seam allowance as before.

Little pinning should be necessary – either butt the seams together or stack the seam allowances. Continue joining rows 1 and 2 in this manner. DO NOT CLIP THE THREADS.

4   Open up the sewn blocks and add the blocks from row 3 onto the edge of row 2, in the same order. Join the quilt in four sections in this manner. After all the blocks are joined in vertical rows, the quilt should be held together by the threads between the rows of blocks. Press the seams between the blocks together in one direction, with the rows of seams running in alternate directions.

5   Join the rows, without clipping the threads, by butting the seams between blocks and lining up all the other piecing as you go. Sew slowly and stitch the rows in alternate directions to avoid stretching. When the four sections of the quilt are completed, join them together in vertical rows.

6   Staystitch ⅛ in (3 mm) from the outside edge of the entire quilt.

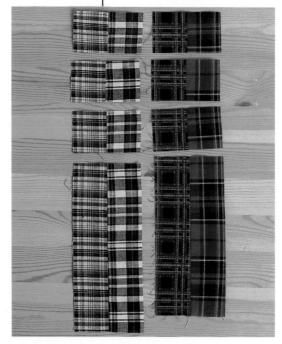

Detail 2: Cut the sewn strips into 2½ in (6 cm) wide sections

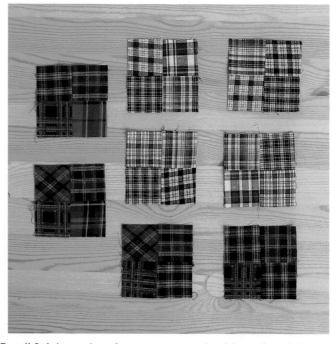

Detail 3: Join sections from one sewn unit with sections from another one

Borders

Add the borders, using the four 6½ (16.5 cm) wide previously cut strips, following the instructions in the "Adding Borders" section in Technical Details on page 13.

Broderie perse

1 Cut out the flowers from the large floral print, leaving a ¼ in (7.5 mm) seam allowance all around.

2 Arrange the flowers in the top left-hand and bottom right-hand corners. Baste the flowers into position, making sure the base is within ½ in (1.5 cm) of the cut edges.

3 Trimming the seam allowance slightly as you go, turn under the raw edges with a needle, and pin them in place. Prepare only a small amount for appliqué at a time.

4 Stitch, using a blind hemming stitch and a thread to match the pieces being applied. You will need to change the thread often, so it is useful to have many needles threaded in the various colors to be used. Try to keep the stitches small, if not invisible.

5 Layer the completed quilt top with the batting and backing in preparation for machine-quilting.

Quilting

1 Quilt diagonally from corner to corner in a straight line through the center of the blocks in one or both directions.

2 Quilt slowly in-the-ditch around the flowers, so they will stand out in relief from the background.

Above: Detail of "Winter Surprise" showing the broderie perse

Binding

Join the previously cut four 2½ in × 85 in (6 cm × 210 cm) strips as necessary to achieve the required lengths for the binding. Add the binding following the instructions in the "Binding" section in Technical Details on page 14.

Noah's Ark

YOU WILL NEED
Note: All fabric quantities are calculated on 44 in (112 cm) wide fabric.
- 2⅞ yd (2.6 m) of the feature-print fabric
- ⅛ yd (10 cm) of twenty-eight different checked fabrics or a total of 1⅓ yd (1.2 m) of assorted checked fabrics
- ⅓ yd (30 cm of striped fabric for the inner border
- 1½ yd (1.3 m) of blue fabric for the outer border and binding OR 3½ yd (1.3 m) of fabric for the border, binding, and backing
- 2⅞ yd (2.6 m) of fabric for the backing
- 50 in x 61 in (128 cm x 156 cm) of batting
- sewing machine
- rotary cutter, mat, and ruler
- thread to blend with the fabrics
- thread to match the backing fabric
- small square ruler
- safety pins
- chalk wheel

Finished size: 46½ in x 57½ in (118 cm x 146 cm)

This simple cot quilt features Debbie Mumm's charming Noah's Ark fabric, with blue and white plaid fabrics joined to make the sashing strips. Many other feature-print fabrics will work just as well. You could use a fabric with autumn leaves, roses or any other large print, with the sashing pieced in complementary colors. The quilt on page 79 has been made in exactly the same way for a strikingly different effect.

Note: It may not be possible to cut the feature print into squares that appear to be absolutely straight. Many prints are not printed exactly on the straight grain. I believe this adds to the charm of the finished quilt and this is one of the reasons I chose checks for the sashing sections – it is impossible to cut most checks so that they look straight. Regardless of the print, make sure your squares are perfectly square and your strips are straight.

Instructions
Note: Use ¼ in (7.5 mm) seam allowances and a smaller than usual stitch.

Cutting and sewing sashing strips
1   From selvage to selvage, cut one strip 1½ in (4 cm) wide from each of the twenty-eight different checked fabrics. If some fabrics are shorter, simply cut an extra strip and join them.
2   Arrange the strips from light to dark (detail 1).
3   Sew the strips from light to dark in groups of four (detail 2), making sure you sew the rows in alternate directions to avoid stretching the fabrics. You should

have seven groups of four (detail 3). Press the seams together in one direction, towards the darker fabric.
4   Cut the sewn strips into 2½ in (6 cm) sections, cutting across the strips (detail 4) to yield seventeen sections from each – 119 in all (110 are needed).
Note: The length of the four sewn strips will determine the size of the feature-print squares. Measure several of your sashing sections to determine this size. If some are a little longer, either trim them or adjust your sewing. Each section should be approximately 4½ in (11.5 cm).

For the feature-print squares
1   From the feature-print fabric, cut forty-eight squares the size of your four sewn strips, approximately 4½ in (11.5 cm).
2   In addition, cut sixty-three 2½ in (6 cm) squares from the feature-print fabric.

Arranging the quilt
On the vertical work surface, arrange the pieced sashing strips randomly, filling in with small and large squares from the feature-print fabric.

Detail 1: Arrange the strips from light to dark

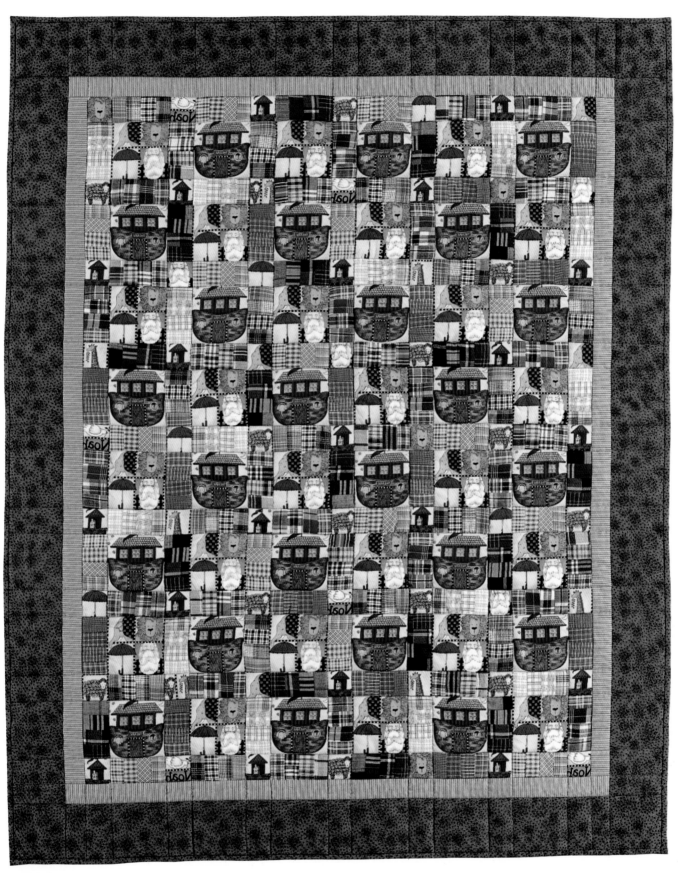

NOAH'S ARK
Judy Turner

Above: A detail of "Noah's Ark" showing the use of the feature print

Constructing the quilt

1 Stack the blocks in rows, beginning at the bottom of the left-hand side. The top left-hand corner block will be on top of the stack. Put a pin in this block to mark the top corner of the quilt and leave the pin in place until the quilt is completed. Stack the second row in the same manner, beginning at the bottom. After this, it is safer to remove only one row at a time, just prior to joining it to the other rows.

2 Beginning with the top two blocks from each stack, chain-piece them, using the same seam allowance as before. Little pinning should be necessary. Continue joining rows 1 and 2 in this manner. DO NOT CLIP THE THREADS.

3 Open up the seam blocks and add the blocks from row 3 to the edge of row 2 in the same order. After all the blocks are joined in vertical rows, the quilt should be held together by the thread between the rows of blocks.

4 Press the seams together in one direction, away from the feature print and towards the sashing sections.

Joining the rows

1 Join the rows without clipping the threads, by butting the seams between the blocks as you go. Sew slowly and stitch the rows in alternate directions to avoid stretching. Press the seams together, in one direction, towards the sashing.

2 Staystitch ⅛ in (3 mm) from the outside edge of the entire quilt.

Borders

1 For the inner border, cut five strips 2 in (5 cm) wide from selvage to selvage. Cut one strip in half, crosswise, and join one half to each of two strips so you have

Detail 2: Sew the strips from light to dark in groups of four

plenty for the length of the quilt. Match the stripe as you join the fabric.

2 For the outer border, cut four strips, lengthwise, 4½ in × 54 in (11.5 cm × 130 cm).

3 Add the borders following the instructions in the "Adding Borders" section in Technical Details on page 13.

4 Layer the completed quilt top with batting and backing in preparation for machine-quilting.

Quilting

1 Read "Preparation for Machine-Quilting" on page 13.

2 Quilt in-the-ditch down either side of the sashing sections in both directions. Use a chalk wheel to mark the continuation of all the quilting lines through the borders.

Binding

1 Cut five strips, lengthwise, 2½ in × 54 in (6 cm × 130 cm), on the straight grain from the border/binding fabric. Join the strips as necessary to achieve the required length.

2 Add the binding following the instructions in the "Binding" section in Technical Details on page 14.

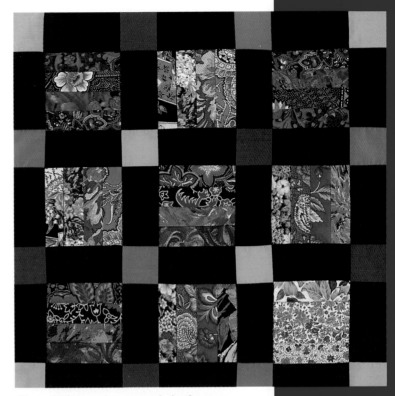

Above: This sample was made in the same way as "Noah's Ark," but this time the squares are pieced and the sashing is a single fabric

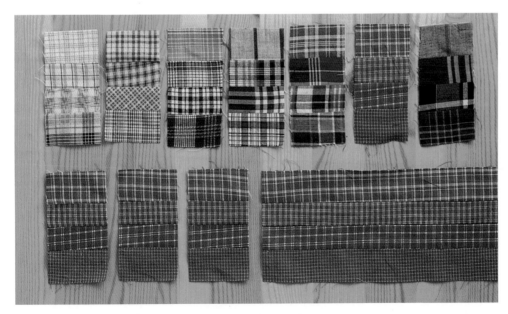

Detail 3 (Top): You should have seven groups of four strips
Detail 4 (Bottom): Cut the sewn strips into 2½ in (6 cm) sections

About the Author

Judy Turner's fascination with color and fabric goes back to her childhood and the influence of her very creative mother. What began as an interest all those years ago has become a passion and a career. These days, Judy can truly be said to be a professional quiltmaker.

She is no doubt one of Australia's best-known quilting teachers, having conducted classes on both sides of the continent and in dozens of places in between. Aside from her quiltmaking, Judy continues to maintain a grueling schedule of traveling and classes, bringing her skill and love of quilting to students in the most remote parts. Her classes are so popular that there seems to be a never-ending list of students eager to participate.

In addition to her teaching, Judy has exhibited her work in numerous exhibitions in America, New Zealand, England, Switzerland, and Japan, and won a great many prizes. "Colorwash Cascade" (page 60) was the joint first prize winner in the theme section of the Sydney Quilt Show in 1993.

Many of Judy's quilts have appeared in print in Australia, the United States and Japan, and she was a featured quilter in *Celebrating the Traditions* (J.B. Fairfax Press 1995). This is the first book that is devoted entirely to her work.

Acknowledgments

To Karen Fail and my editor, July Poulos, from J.B. Fairfax Press, many thanks for inviting me to write a book, for believing I could, and for making it happen.

To photographer, Andrew Payne, many thanks for doing a superb job.

My sincere thanks to my friend and mentor, Margaret Rolfe, who has supported and advised me since we first met. It was she who encouraged me to teach, opening the door wide in ways I never could have imagined.

I'd like to thank the members of Canberra Quilters for the friendship, encouragement and the fun we share. Being part of such a dynamic group has been exciting and inspiring, as well as providing a network of caring people who constantly support one another.

I am indebted to my friend and student, Julie Wells, who typed the manuscript and in so doing gave me the time to complete the quilts, as well as sharing many other aspects of the writing of this book.

To friends Barbara Goddard, Ruth Keys, and Margaret Rolfe, my sincere thanks for their hand-finishing of several quilts, and to Ros Jackson, Kay McDougall, and Beth Miller, many thanks for their advice. Thanks also to my students who have taught me so much, especially Anieta Barendricht, Lilija Brown, Marcia Jackson, and Sandy Lew, who have kindly loaned their quilts.

Many thanks to my son, Nicholas, for his practical help and creative input, and to my daughter, Alison, for typing, hand-finishing, and gifts of flowers. My heartfelt thanks to my husband, Ian, for his love and support in every possible way, making him not only the world's best cook but the world's best husband.

Judy